Advance Praise for
Potluck

"Spagna peels back the reality of living in a small, close community. It is not easy. It is full of tensions that never resolve. Full of differences, sacrifices, and rewards. In the end Spagna wins through to unforgettable clarity about this oft-glamorized, easily sentimental condition—clarity that feels like wisdom."
    —David Oates, author of *City Limits*

"So many writers romanticize rural life, and so few address its true difficulties and rewards. Ana Maria Spagna never flinches: In this wry, wise, and beautifully written collection of essays, she takes a deep, honest look at her life in a small community, and teaches all of us something about ourselves and our neighbors."
    —Michelle Nijhuis, Contributing Editor, *High Country News*

"From one of the country's most remote hamlets comes one of the West's most perceptive and lyrical literary voices. Ana Maria Spagna's powerful prose seamlessly integrates the Big Three of quality writing: education, edification, and entertainment. Few place-based writers can pull that off. Ana Maria pulls it off brilliantly. Her work belongs on the same shelf as Mary Sojourner and Ellen Meloy. It's that good."
    —M. John Fayhee, Editor, the *Mountain Gazette* and author of *Bottoms Up*

T0099397

Potluck

Community on the Edge of Wilderness

Ana Maria Spagna

Oregon State University Press

Corvallis

The paper in this book meets the guidelines for permanence and durability of the Committee on Production Guidelines for Book Longevity of the Council on Library Resources and the minimum requirements of the American National Standard for Permanence of Paper for Printed Library Materials Z39.48-1984.

Library of Congress Cataloging-in-Publication Data
Spagna, Ana Maria.
  Potluck : community on the edge of wilderness / Ana Maria Spagna.
    p. cm.
  ISBN 978-0-87071-591-4 (alk. paper)
  1. Spagna, Ana Maria. 2. United States. National Park Service.--Officials and employees--Biography. 3. Mountain life--Washington (State)--Stehekin. 4. Stehekin (Wash.)--Social life and customs. 5. Stehekin (Wash.)--Biography. I. Title.
  F899.S84S73 2011
  979.7'59--dc22

                                                          2010049243

© 2011 Ana Maria Spagna
All rights reserved.
First published in 2011 by Oregon State University Press
Printed in the United States of America

 Oregon State University Press
121 The Valley Library
Corvallis OR 97331-4501
541-737-3166 • fax 541-737-3170
http://oregonstate.edu/dept/press

Dedicated to the memory of Phillip L. Garfoot 1937-2010

"Never show weakness"

It sounds like a tough guy maxim,
but it comes with a generous dose of compassion.

Contents

Potluck

Tables—sheets of plywood, actually, set atop saw horses—line the center of the Stehekin Community Hall that on Sundays serves as the Pentecostal church. The tables are over-crowded with chicken enchiladas, Swedish meatballs, organic salad greens, pasta with sun-dried tomatoes, dishes as varied and predictable as the sixty of us who sit on wooden benches waiting to eat. We've gathered on this November evening to bid farewell to a family that's moving. The day has been gray, as have been the past several, ever since an inversion settled into the valley and effectively erased the peaks so that the conifers stand out darkly, nearly black, against the gray, and leafless hardwood limbs divide the gray into twisted foreboding shapes, and the river runs over gray granite boulders, and the sameness grows oppressive. We needed, all of us, to get out of the house, to get a little change of scenery, to share some food and company, to be together. The kids feel it, and they romp excitedly in the tree-hemmed parking lot in the slopover glow from the hall windows. And the adults feel it, too. The woodstove has heated the crowded room shirt-sleeve warm, and the mood is cheery if slightly restrained.

Between aged log posts, black-and-white photos dating back to the turn of the last century adorn the walls. They're posed community shots, grainy and indistinct. Some of the faces are younger versions of folks here tonight; others are ancestors of people here tonight whose camera-caught characteristics—large ears, toothy grins, a certain prideful tip of the head—identify

9

We laughed. After several years of living up here full-time, I sometimes forget what it's like to live in what people insistently call "the real world." Stehekin has no town council, which is probably one reason we manage to get along. A locally elected school board governs the one-room school, and grudges bred on the school board sometimes simmer for decades. Without an institution to tether us, our union is tenuous. You can tell by the looks of us: long gray beards and military haircuts, cowboy boots and sandals. We wear our cultural/political beliefs literally on our sleeves as if we glean identity from the glossy catalogs in our post office boxes: wool vs. fleece, cowboy hats vs. ball caps, Cabelas vs. REI.

We spoon dollops of this, dabs of that onto paper plates, food that will likely meld in my gut later and set off alarms. I am not completely at ease here, I admit. Decorum rules the day, politeness born of our differences and our overarching respect for privacy. One friend's only son has recently gone off to college, and she is sad. Another friend is newly pregnant, uncertain and sick. Yet another teeters on the brink of divorce. Tonight we do not speak of such troubles. Here we are bound together by something more superficial, and also much deeper: a cold night, a family leaving.

This family is following the career path that requires upwardly mobile park rangers to move to a different park every three years or so. The idea is familiar: best to have professionals with broad and varied experience, able to apply big abstract management concepts to small places. In general, permanent Park Service families are earnest and dedicated, if a little neurotic. They get to see the prettiest places on earth, live there for a while, then move on. Many of them come to Stehekin as a stepping stone. They resent their tenure here and tick off the long weeks in purgatory.

In contrast, the family that is leaving this time liked it here, and they're leaving as much to be closer to their families back East as for any other reason. The father is a law-enforcement officer of the Andy Griffith mold, who prefers a chat to a confrontation, and is well liked in the valley. His wife raises search-and-rescue dogs; we'd see her mornings on the road running the border collies, one who died here, and one who will move with them. Their daughter arrived as a long-lashed toddler and leaves now as a long-legged and confident girl who, in springtime, runs with packs of kids out on the wide mud flats at the head of the lake. The family would have liked to stay, but like major league ball players, permanent Park Service employees can't afford to get too attached to any one place.

This kind of life, ripe with heartbreak, is, of course, more norm than exception. Upwardly mobile or desperately downwardly so, Americans move an average of twelve times in a lifetime. Every place, really, is the Way Through. You bring what you have to offer. You fill your plate with what is there. You eat, and then you leave. There is privilege in movement: a richness of experience. (Another trail crew buddy once found a copy of the *Utne Reader* in his bunkhouse shortly after moving to the Pacific Northwest from Texas. "Well, I've been broadened," he said. And he had.) But there is disconnect, too.

I should know. I lived much of my adult life as a seasonal— moving semi-annually from place to place—and I remember how it feels to know you'll soon be gone: the less I do, the less I hurt. On the land. In myself. During wildfires, I remained coldly detached. Philosophy dictated my response: let it burn. Ditto for floods: let the wild river run. Ever since I decided to stay put, I no longer have that luxury. Now during natural disasters, I'm too worried about my neighbors' homes to ponder philosophy. If it's disconcerting, this weight of responsibility, this heavy plate of mix-and-match food, it's also comforting. My neighbors, after all, worry about my home too.

The room is growing warmer yet and more crowded as latecomers straggle in. A few Park Service mucky-mucks have traveled ten hours—six by car, four by boat—to be here for the farewell celebration. They arrive bearing plastic trays of veggies, chips and salsa, boxes of Franzia wine, though wine, usually, is a no-no in this sometimes church building. And the crowd seems genuinely glad to have them.

When I was a kid in the seventies, potlucks were a way of life. We had church picnics and neighborhood swim parties and annual potlucks in the school auditorium that offered parents the chance to meet and offered us kids the chance to eat Kentucky Fried Chicken from the bucket. We elbowed ahead in the line like Dickens characters, like starving orphans, when actually we were the precise opposite: we were safe and insulated, spoiled, and utterly uninhibited. It was perfect practice, I sometimes think, for living in Stehekin. Then again, potlucks happen everywhere. This morning I was listening to a radio call-in show from the small apple-orchard town downlake when a woman called about the annual high school football team potluck. She reminded listeners that there would be a lot of folks in attendance and that some of them would be football players—more than forty kids on the three teams: Freshman, JV, Varsity. Her message was clear: bring plenty.

Outside, thick icy sludge coats every limb. One crashed onto our new woodshed roof last night. Cottonwood leaves, spade shaped, playing-card sized, still green, stick straight up in the slop, melting now to ankle-deep pools. All night rain spattered on the cabin roof like the enthusiastic applause at a political convention, causing the icy slabs to slide off the dormer with startling irregular thuds. Around here in summer social life grows rich and abundant as the deciduous trees—maples, ash, dogwoods—and the lush gardens and wild berries. If I want to go to a potluck every night I can. I can bring a bucket of beer and sit by a campfire, laughing and swatting mosquitoes. Summer is frenetic. In winter, silence pervades. You must get very close to the river, barely a trickle, to hear its flow. At home, we can no longer stand the buzz of the computer, or the freezer kicking on in the night, or the kathump of snow off the roof.

These things, the most real and raw, are what we share. I picture my roots intertwining with the others who are here tonight because, well, we are here. A few years back a job came open that required negotiating land trades and dictating land-use rules, and the managers told me frankly not to bother to apply, that I wouldn't be able to separate myself—untangle myself—from the community enough to make the right decisions. I knew it was true. I've become so entangled, in fact, that I'm beginning to think it's a good thing.

And I'm not alone. I recently took an informal email poll of friends in their mid-thirties like I am. Some live in big cities and some, like me, live in small backwoodsy communities. Some live in their home towns, having stayed or returned, and some live impossibly far, geographically and culturally, from where they grew up. Turns out they all attend potlucks or dinner parties at roughly the same rate as I do: for sports teams or book clubs, for church or for school. In our twenties, belonging meant searching out the places and the people that melded best to the version of life that we aspired to. And what joy in finding them. High jinks! Now wherever we are, we meld ourselves, or some part of ourselves, to the communities we find ourselves in. As best we can. When I was a kid, my stomach acted up at potlucks. I remember the familiar acid curdling that meant "I want to go home." Usually it was because there were too many people I didn't know. Nowadays, no matter how happy I am to be settled where I am, I sometimes want to go home from potlucks because there are too many people I *do* know.

The last eaters are interrupted by a loud shrill whistle. Time for the formalities. Speeches are given, brief but heartfelt. A couple that has recently acquired a tiny touristy outdoor-supply store comes forward with a new backpack for the eight-year-old. My trail crew boss, Phil Garfoot, a permanent park employee who's chosen to live here for thirty years, brings forward a hand-carved wooden arrowhead, the symbol of the National Park Service. A descendant of the original settlers, whose relatives crowd the photos on the walls, offers a wooden bow hewn from the plentiful local maple. The ranger thanks them, teeters on the edge of tears, and steps back into the shadows. His daughter doesn't bother with stoicism. She stands before us sobbing softly while her closest eight-year-old pals hover near the door, waiting for all this to be over so they can go back outside and play.

I'm moved by the scene. Who wouldn't be? I'm sad for the family, but I'm also humbled by the way my neighbors have learned over time the graceful art of making friends and letting them go. They invite new seasonals and summer folks to dinner. They make small talk in the post office even when maybe they'd rather—just once, for godsake!—be anonymous. They gladly welcomed the family that is leaving, and they are sad to see them go. I aspire to their combination of openness and steadfastness. That, after all, is the rest of the potluck story, isn't it? You bring what you have to offer. You fill your plate with what is there. You eat and then you leave. But while you're there, you hope for warmth and light, courtesy and generosity. And after a while, you learn to bring more than your share.

Eventually dishes are cleared and claimed. It's time to go.

Stepping out into the moonless dark, Laurie and I realize too late that we've forgotten a flashlight, so we navigate by the sound of nearby Rainbow Creek. This must be the right way, we think. No, this must. It's a guessing game, terrifying and hysterically funny, a lostness not too different from the long journey that has brought the two of us, alone and together, to this potluck tonight. We drag our fingertips along slushy needles and twigs until we hit the ragged solid edge of asphalt. For now, we're sure where we are and that we're safe. Again. Still. So we get in the car, and we drive away.

Thirteen Percent Catholic

Sunday morning. The paper-thin gray of a favorite old T-shirt spreads across the sky. Ocean haze has spilled inland off the Pacific across sixty long miles to Riverside, and Mass has ended after ninety long minutes at Our Lady of Perpetual Help. Our Lady sits behind a faux iron fence on the corner of two four-lane streets—wide and nondescript—that harbor the faint odor of a recent agricultural past. Across one street, a large blue farmhouse is surrounded by newly built tract homes in earth tones. Down the other, a white stucco convent built for twenty nuns nowadays houses four. A large crowd mills about the fountain, exchanging news and hugs, always hugs, and small children scurry underfoot. No one is in a hurry to leave. The haze burns off, and heat radiates off the parking lot in translucent waves like those announcing a dream sequence on TV. I'm twelve years old, and I have an idea for a novel.

The Parish will be an ambitious novel like *Roots* maybe or like *Centennial*. The storyline will follow the interconnected lives of diverse characters coming together with the help of one charismatic priest: Father Dominic DePasquale. Father De is real, and his name translates to mean Easter, my mother never fails to tell me. Easter, she says. Like resurrection. And I know why: because for our family, Father De represents just that.

Before we went to Our Lady, we'd attended church at a seminary outside town. Often as not, newly ordained priests celebrated Mass outdoors. The music was upbeat, and the young priests kept the liturgy lively. When, afterwards, we drove down the hill onto a car-crowded avenue, past the gray industrial Rohr factory and numerous liquor stores separated by empty lots, tire shops, taco wagons, we descended into dryness and disarray, and when, in the late 1970s, Mass was no longer celebrated at the seminary—too few recruits—we landed back at our regular diocesan parish, Our Lady, in time for two momentous events. My father died of a massive heart attack while out jogging. And Father De arrived as the new pastor.

I sat through my dad's funeral at Our Lady staring at the crucifix suspended by wires above the altar and the coffin, so terrifyingly life-like: sinewy and bloodied, head bowed with the crown of thorns, and nails, too, driven through his palms and between the tendons atop his crossed feet. After Father De arrived, a huge modern tapestry appeared behind the altar of the risen Christ with arms outstretched. If the hanging didn't exactly supplant the crucifix, it certainly outshone it. The tapestry was four or fives times as large and far more vibrant. Try to focus on Jesus with the sword-pierced rib cage, say, and you'd be distracted by swirling orange and gold. The tapestry was cubist in style, not the least bit life-life. Or death-like, I should say. Which was precisely the point.

Father De was a very short man, short as me, with dark curly hair. One on one, he was gentle and thoughtful, quick with a hug or a brief touch, his hands often turned outward by his side, his fingers splayed, in a posture that suggested both openness and restlessness. Yes, yes, a hug, but not too long, not too hard. I am here for you when you need me, his demeanor suggested, but not perhaps beyond that. He did not laugh easily, though he often smiled; he did not drink heavily, though he did not decline a glass of wine. But he would've made a lousy protagonist for my novel, I now think, because I didn't really know a thing about him. The plain truth is that there was nothing very exciting about Father De. What was exciting was what he preached.

Community, he said. We must become a community. Not community in the civic sense: say the pledge and join the parade. Community like St. Francis intended, or maybe even like Marx: live simply, renounce materialism, fight oppression. Father De's politics were clear, leaning hard left in the Reagan era, but his main message was closer to home: people should depend on each other and care for each other, actively and outwardly. While some parishioners were offended and left to attend one of the more palatial and palatable saint-named churches across town, others—unexpected stolid unhip types—endured and even embraced the changes. One white-bunned widow who stayed offered the same petition aloud every single Sunday.

"For all of our children, particularly those who have fallen away from the Church," she'd say.

We kids giggled at the predictability of Humpty Dumpty falling away from the church Sunday after Sunday, then shattering in an eggshell heap.

It was an anomaly, I know, a glitch in time to be raised Catholic in California post-Vatican II and pre-John Paul II. Catholicism was clearly divided; even as a kid I could see that: baroque vs. cubist, stained glass vs. macramé, Ave Maria vs. Kumbaya. Often as not, since nearly all of our Catholic relatives lived in St. Louis, this rift took on a distinctly geographic character. Church in St. Louis felt rigid and insular, but self-assured. Our great-uncle Charlie was archbishop of Kansas City and lived in a mansion where, when we visited, he let us run wild, tracing our fingertips around crystal cereal bowls to see if they would sing, spinning the oversized globe in the library to see how fast it would go, while he smiled, this regal man, ever beneficent. My Irish grandmother, in her later years, responded to the refrains at Mass in her cigarette-rasped brogue, "Lard, have mercy," and we laughed. Sometimes she waited to respond a half-second later than the rest of the congregation, so we would laugh some more. Midwestern Catholicism was more conservative—no guitars, no hugs, no hand holding for the Our Father, no clapping and/or sign-language arm waving for the Alleluia—and less emotionally fraught, but it didn't offer the comfort that Father De's community did.

Really, the community, as Father De coined it, was just a group of friends. Nothing out of the ordinary. Other people had close circles of friends from their jobs or their distant hometowns or their country clubs, and they didn't bother to call themselves a community. That ours did struck me, even then, as a little self-important. But who was it hurting? I loved belonging to the community. The parishioners were earnest and faithful, easy and generous, and we gathered often for pool parties or work parties—once renovating an entire house for a large family—or for baptism celebrations for children and adults alike who'd been dunked in a makeshift fountain in a most un-Catholic way. Many of the parishioners had young children, and I babysat for a dollar an hour, thick wads of cash that I shoved in an envelope under my mattress, saving for when I could move away.

On my bedroom floor, I sketched Father De's figure on construction paper, the cover of my novel-to-be, in his white robes with his arms outstretched like Jesus. I pictured diverse and colorful characters. It was the era of rainbows, and they seemed to pop up everywhere: stickers on my night light, decals on T-shirts, even murals on the walls at the Jazzercise studio in the shopping mall across town. When I imagined my novel, rainbows are what I saw. *The Parish*. About what? I didn't know. I only knew that I believed what Father De said: take care of one another, forgive transgressions, and include the oddballs—even when that meant holding Tommy Turkowski's hand during the Our Father—because the oddball, often as not, turns out to be you.

Though most of the families in the community were younger than ours, one family had a daughter my age, and our shy friendship blossomed one Sunday afternoon when we listened to *Jesus Christ Superstar* at her house. Her house was largish and set back among acres of orange groves, with a yard of tall eucalyptus and pepper trees, shady and pungent and cool, like the set for a Western. Inside the house, Julie put the soundtrack on the record player, and from there the drama unfolded organically: I whipped my arms wide crucifixion-style while I berated my Father in heaven, and Julie—aka Mary Magdalene—sashayed in to oil my feet. Then I was Judas not wanting blood money, and she was the rocking Superstar Himself. Our impromptu performance was fluid and dramatic; we were nearly teenagers, oddballs of the first degree, and our friendship was cemented for life. These days we keep in touch via email, and a few months back Julie sent me an Internet quiz that measures how closely your core spiritual beliefs match up with those of particular religions. (Since it's a correlation, not a pie chart, you can be, say, 75 percent Baptist and 90 percent Secular Humanist at the same time.) According to Belief-O-Matic, these days Julie is 90 percent Buddhist, 90 percent Unitarian. Me, I'm 100 percent Quaker. And only 13 percent Catholic.

Still, my adult home is adorned with Catholic trinkets. Family photos show Great-uncle Charlie in bishop's garb, and his sister, Reginald, in Sally Field-style nun garb, even though, except for on TV, I've never seen such a get-up. By the time I hit catechism, nuns wore plain black skirts and white blouses. The bookshelf holds a small chipped statue of St. Francis I've had since kindergarten. The bathroom sports a campy Virgin Mary nightlight. I wear Catholicism like a caricaturized lost ethnic identity—about as Catholic as a green McDonald's shake is Irish, as Olive Garden is Italian—but the fact that I own up to it at all betrays stubborn loyalty, and something deeper, too.

Only after many years did I come to realize that community was not Father De's personal crusade, but a buzz word copped directly from the precepts of Vatican II and a concept as familiar to my parents as an old rug. Yet another priest was a regular visitor to our home, a priest so radical he'd more or less been kicked out of his own order. What he mainly did was travel Latin America, and barring that, the state of California, staying in guest rooms. He had been at Berkeley for the Free Speech movement. Now, he championed the Sandinistas. Poets, he cried. Poets running the government. Imagine. Just as it should be! At Berkeley, he'd helped start a summer program modeled after the Peace Corps called Amigos Anonymous that worked on small-scale development projects in Mexico. Sometimes the priest frightened me. Over dinner, he taunted me when I didn't rise to the pitch of his political enthusiasm, calling me "blasé" and demanding that I refill his bourbon glass. I held my tongue from rebuke. I knew to accept him because of Amigos Anonymous, of course, and because I knew he needed a safety net.

He was not the only one. On Saturdays, I climbed through a hole in the cinder-block wall that separated Our Lady from an open weedy field to play on the parish softball team for seventh-grade girls. I'd always been athletic, but I'd lost my edge. I swung hard, but couldn't connect. I ran my heart out, but I couldn't slide, ever. The pitcher was a straight-haired girl with a sneer who whipped her arm clockwise in a wild fury and sent the ball whizzing past hesitant, unsuspecting batters like me. The coach, a beer-drinking neighbor, clearly held disdain for me. I wasn't sure why. Because of my height—too little? Or my weight—too much? Or, more likely, for my status: a favored student, a goody two-shoes. I was, I think, too effete, too uncertain and self-involved for softball, but I stuck with it. For love of the game? Hardly. I liked the late-afternoon sun in smog-hued orange and red, and I liked the evening air and the evening out. Evening at home could be problematic. I missed my dad, and for reasons I couldn't yet understand, I was baffled by puberty, so usually I sequestered myself in my bedroom listening to the Beatles—long after they'd broken up—on the turntable, rereading the liner notes. Then on Saturday I'd walk to Our Lady for the afternoon game and stay late to wander aimless circles around the fountain, waiting for Sunday.

For a while, after I gave up softball, I took up dancing at church. The leader, dark haired and svelte, gypsy-like in her spirituality, looked as if she ought to be in a room full of candles with tarot cards. She introduced sacred dance, yet another newfangled concept, and for a few weeks in preparation for brief Sunday performances, we practiced yoga, breathing in and out, and we paraded up and down the aisles past the Stations of the Cross, making broad gestures. And though I was a cloddy graceless sort, who walked with the gait of a teenage boy, slouchy and reticent, I loved sacred dance. I breathed in and out, and thought about eternity. I got my driver's license, and as high school wore on I tried to cling to my faith as a bulwark against everything around me—the blandly conservative Reagan years, the new mall with the pretzel stand with the too-rich cream cheese where pregnant girls worked once they quit school—but I was losing my grip.

The Catholic high school I attended hung smack in the middle of the whole uneasy balance. Our teachers were former nuns and recent college graduates who could get jobs without credentials. Our principal had ties to Palm Springs Cadillac dealerships and drank midday at a seedy bar tucked between Big 5 and Carl's Jr. Scotty, the vice president of our class, who wore ties to school and kept his hair shorter than any teenager had in a yearbook decade, was rumored to be facing charges for grand theft auto. When our sophomore English teacher threatened to fail him, he stole her grade book. After the fact that she was our only black teacher spawned a complicated series of lawsuit threats, Scotty hardly received a hand slap.

My mother begged me to switch to public school. She'd returned to graduate school by then, and she was taking courses in liberation theology, and the focus on social justice did not mesh well, I suppose, with used Cadillacs and racist lawsuits. I resented her suggestion because I didn't want to leave my friends, but also because, after a while, I didn't share her idealism. An actor for president, an actor for pope, and on the nightly news, Tom Brokaw insisting that the U.S. was not funding the contras. Who to believe? At church, we saw a documentary about four dead American nuns with gruesome footage of a dismembered hand in the jungle. At home, we learned how Archbishop Oscar Romero had been murdered in El Salvador while he celebrated Mass. But on talk radio, we began to hear the rallying cry that has not abated since: what America faces is a crisis of values, and rosary in hand, John Paul II echoed the sentiment. My mother remained steadfast. Me, I wavered. I could not believe that Oscar Romero's martyrdom would lead to a renewal of Vatican II values any more than Kennedy's assassination had renewed faith in government, or King's had invigorated civil rights, or John Lennon's had led to a jaunty reunion of the other three lads, for that matter. At school, Scotty criticized the Sandinistas.

"They're not saints, you know. They're oppressive, too," he said.

"No they're not," I insisted, appalled. Poets! I wanted to cry. They're poets!

Scotty had the bemused laugh of the powerful. "How do you know?"

"I know people who've been there," I said. For once in my life I'd take a stand.

"Oh yeah, well, OK," he smirked.

When, a few short years later, I learned about Sandinista censorship of *La Prensa* and oppression of indigenous people,

I was devastated. I would have taken the news better that the virgin birth had been a grand hoax.

Here's the truth. I'm ambivalent, at best, about the central tenets of Catholicism: the Virgin Birth, the Trinity, even Jesus Christ as Lord and Savior. I'm content to shrug and let the mysteries stand. I'm opposed to much of the tradition of the Catholic Church—the role of women, the attitude toward homosexuality and birth control—and I'm flabbergasted by what both tenet and tradition so often fail to address: the godliness of Nature. But I've landed in a makeshift community that governs itself by precisely the same code that Father De preached: take care of one another, forgive transgressions, include the oddball. And Belief-O-Matic says I'm only 13 percent Catholic? Belief-O-Matic does not know everything.

By the time I left for college, I could look back without the rainbow lens to see the parish through Joan Didion's eyes. Those characters I wanted to write about so badly weren't particularly diverse; they were regular working-class thirty-somethings who commuted in the predawn hours to Orange County or LA to work as construction supervisors and salesmen of small electronic parts, who wore jeans and shorts to church, quintessential Californians. It took longer for me to see the church askance. I tried living in a Catholic co-op for a while, but found, ironically enough, that living around that many people—living in community for real—did not work for me. I needed space and solitude and lacked the words for explaining that need, and soon I left. I wandered into the wilderness, and just kept walking.

Sometimes I read tragic novels about indigenous people giving up their ancient ways because the culture changed too fast around them, and sometimes—though it's crazy—I think that's what happened to us. By the late 1970s California, like the rest of the U.S., had undergone remarkable unfathomable change, both the TV sound-bite sort—Bobby Kennedy, Charles Manson, Patty Hearst—and a more subtle and pervasive suburban version. So many kids I knew had divorced parents that, before my dad died, I desperately wished mine would divorce too, the way other kids wished for braces or leg casts. My parents had believed with all their hearts that stodgy Catholicism, the casual white-bread Midwestern version, did not stand a chance. Turns out, maybe they had it backwards. Most California Catholics were immigrants, Vietnamese and Mexican, who had no use for three-chord anthem hymns, and most of the younger white folks who preferred a more upbeat service chose to attend the new evangelical mega-church out by the Kmart.

Sometimes, too—and this is the creepier analogy—I think about fundamentalism, how it bristles against mainstream culture, how it claims to be the truest branch of whatever faith spawned it. Sometimes I tell myself that is precisely what I was taught, what I believed, in my heart of hearts: that we were the chosen ones. With that in mind, maybe it's best that we fell so hard. If we did. The last time I attended Mass in St. Louis, in the mid-1990s, I was stunned to see hand-waving Alleluias and hugs aplenty. Maybe, I thought, there's no "we" about it. Maybe it's just me, fallen away from the church, in my eggshell heap.

Shortly after I left for college, Father De left Our Lady, not because of scandal or politics—that's the expected denouement, I know, the sordid one, the senseless tragic undercurrent of all that lovey-dovey seventies business—but to become a hospital chaplain working with AIDS patients. A new immigrant priest arrived at Our Lady who pronounced virgin "weer-gin" and made us laugh like we'd laughed at our grandmother, and suddenly church was just church again: conservative, hierarchical, blasé, sometimes plain silly. The parting was made easy. But not complete.

These days, I try to hold fast to Father De's legacy. Community. The word holds the sheen of Sunday morning sunshine coming in through my bedroom window past the oranges hanging on limbs overripe; we never picked them because they were Valencias, not Navels, not as sweet or as easy to get as the ones at the store. When, these days, my neighbors in Stehekin use the C word—and they do so often—I flinch, embarrassed by the familiar self-importance. But I also know what it can do, that C word, how it can offer a bulwark against a world full of sadness. This is what we have. This is what will survive the political upheavals, clashes of generation and geography, and maybe even religion: that hope is not an individual feeling.

Most years around Christmas I return to my mother's house to sit on the backyard steps in shorts, soaking in the pure undeserved grace of winter sun. A couple years ago, we threw her a birthday party. My mother does not attend church at Our Lady anymore, but the more progressive Newman Center. She does work at Our Lady's busy food pantry every Monday, with old friends, passing out paper sacks with peanut butter and bread and tuna and dry milk. God knows the world has changed in the past thirty years every bit as much as it ever did, and these stalwart boomers shrug and go about their routines. Their community spirit is ordinary, non-exclusive, and contagious. For all my youthful piety, I am very nearly ashamed that, apparently, the best I can do for this troubled world is hide in the woods, doing as little harm as possible.

At the party, Father De sits in the center of the room, stooped over a cane, suffering now in the late stages of diabetes. I haven't seen him in twenty years, but he seems to remember me, as my mother's daughter at least, as part of the fold. He smiles, and for the first time I notice deeply etched crows feet by his tiny black eyes and hope against hope that he has known happiness at least some of the time. I try, but fail, to think of something appropriate to say. I hold his hand tightly for a moment, then he pulls me close to peck my cheek.

"You're a good girl," he says.

I stand upright, and I watch as I let go his hand, how his aged fingers splay by his side, close, then spread again, ever restless. And ever open.

La Linea

Barbed wire pulls taut across the desert and binds us together. A few hours ago you could see *la linea*, the line it draws, as the sun sank mercifully away. One side green from well-traveled waters, the other a yellower shade of brown. One side crowded with assembly plants and abandoned pickups, the other covered by fields of strawberries and artichokes. Wet, dry. Cluttered, cleared. Dirty, clean. Rich, poor. Now it is dark and the distinctions are lost. The Argus stands alone, one pink stucco building along the farm access road two hundred meters north of the border, the only establishment of any sort within walking distance of the abandoned barracks where we live, and the only bar for miles. We sit on torn vinyl chairs, segregated by table: sandals here, dress shoes at the bar, work boots in the corner. For a moment, helicopter searchlights filter through the dust-coated window. Then they are gone. The bartender glances up from a game of solitaire. One of the Mexicans chooses "La Bamba" on the jukebox and begins shuffling about the room in heavy boots, bobbing his head, sloshing his beer. Someone just said that Crazy Ray is getting married. Here. Tonight.

"Who the Hell is Ray?" one of the border patrol officers, still uniformed, asks loudly.

"Hell if I know," mumbles the bartender.

"*¿Quien es el loco?*" Try the other language.

"That old guy, lives out there alone," a Mexican answers in English.

I glance around to gauge the tension. Maybe it's time for me to leave.

Leave well enough alone, I should have. Three years I'd spent at college in Oregon, glorious Oregon, green green grass and blue skies, a short drive to the Cascade volcanoes, or along a curvy fern-lined road to the Pacific, where, in winter, storms sent spray from atop cresting waves, row after row of them, and you could stand alone on the beach with sand pelting your face and think big thoughts. In town I rode my bike daily to and from work—teaching swimming lessons to disabled kids—in the sun along the river and in the rain among the fir trees, needles dripping and mossy, miraculous. I had not grown sick of the place, not even close, unless it was a kind of lovesickness. The longer I stayed, the longer I wanted to stay. But that summer I left. I had no choice. As a literature student, I was given to big thoughts, and as a lifelong Catholic, my big thoughts led to guilt, and when I was twenty years old guilt led me, against my better judgment, to Tijuana, the busiest port of entry in the world, to work in orphanages for a small non-profit agency called, simply, Los Niños. And to the Argus.

A shaggy-bearded blond gestures toward the darkened window with a foaming bottle of Corona. "He's that biker that stays behind the old barracks, keeps to himself."

The border cop grins. "There's nothing but trash behind those barracks."

"Hey, Crazy Ray fixes those bikes he collects back there, then sells them at the auction in San Ysidro. You ask me it's a more honest living than most *americanos* make, you know?"

I return to my solitude, embarrassed. I ache sometimes for the long California-girl summers I spent running through the sprinklers. "What do you want to be when you grow up?" my parents used to ask.

"Tan and blond and strong," I always answered, and I meant it.

Q

In my memory, Tijuana is universally gray. Ocean haze melds with bus exhaust and frenetic activity. I carried a water bottle and wore khaki pants in the stifling heat so as not to offend the conservative sensibilities of middle-class Mexicans, though I really ought to have been wearing a dress, and midweek I rode city buses for ten pesos, less than a nickel at the time, and I almost always had to stand, to reach on tiptoes for the overhead bar, as the crowded bus lurched through the city and I tried to make sense of the world around me.

The problem was not what you'd expect, not what it ought to have been, or not entirely so. Not just the cardboard shacks along the river bottom that would be flooded every year by nature or intent. Not just the long-lashed toddlers in the orphanages or the maimed beggars in the storefronts, but the whole of it: the insensibly loud city, the silent proud *abuelas* on the bus, stockings rolled to the ankles, the cat-calling *chicos* on the streets, the gaudy tourist booths and the gaudy tourists themselves, the trash-strewn outskirts, and the upper-class neighborhoods surrounded by stucco walls with broken glass embedded atop them and bougainvilleas draped over them, places that seemed both far too elegant and far too shabby for what they were. At Los Niños, twenty of us lived in the barracks next to the Argus on the American side. Some of us were summer help and some were year-rounders, and we all volunteered in Tijuana all day every day in exchange for room and board. We ate communally, vegetarian usually, and drove vans across the border early each morning to work. On weekends we hosted American high school kids, who also ate communally and crossed the border daily. They did a little work, sure, like we did, but the main point was to introduce them to the realities of the Third World (we still called it that) generally, and of Tijuana uniquely: the cardboard shacks and the beggars, the *maquiladoras* sprouting up and exploiting child labor, the eerily silent orphanages where babies never cried because it did no good.

Back in the barracks at night, after a meatless spaghetti supper, we gave informal talks on international relations—thinly veiled socialist treatises and plain unavoidable truths—the PRI, the World Bank, the whole wide world complicit to these heinous crimes. Much as I agreed with the politics, I was growing uncomfortable with the professed simplicity. In each of the neighborhoods we visited, there were well-known families who changed religion or political affiliation at the drop of a hat to get more of whatever was being offered—food, clothing, pencils, balloons. Today a social democrat, tomorrow a Mormon. The proud Mexican kids at the orphanage playing soccer fist-fought over which team got to be the U.S., which had to be Mexico. Labels were interchangeable, meaningless. American. Mexican. Officer. Activist. Across all these clear bold lines, the vagaries of human nature freely crossed, and young as I was I could not wrap my mind around the complexities of this, of how humans interact with each other, the stark contrast of what we purport to believe and how we live.

A motorcycle pulls up, a Harley. Crazy Ray jumps off and stomps into the Argus with a growl. It's the first time I've seen him up close. He's big, six-four or more, wearing heavy riding boots and Levi's, shirtless except for a leather vest that shows his graying chest hair. His forearms are coated with bicycle grease. A salt-and-pepper beard reaches down to his belt line but doesn't mask the sun-roughened cheekbones or the furrowed brow. His hair is pulled back in a bushy ponytail topped by a faded ball cap. The cap reads: *Rosarito is for Lovers*. This must be the first time anyone around here has seen him up close because the Argus falls silent while Crazy Ray leans against the doorway picking dirt from under his fingernails, examining the decor, and eyeing the crowd with amusement. Or contempt. He grunts, turns, and disappears on the Harley into the dark.

"It must be true," the shaggy beard announces, and a murmur of excitement follows. The bartender searches for champagne.

I glance over at my coworkers. Someone must have run back to the barracks with news of a happening. The crowd has grown, and they shout eagerly to one another and kick a worn hacky sack that occasionally lands near the jukebox. When it does, one of the dancing Mexicans flicks it back.

α

My coworkers at Los Niños, especially the year-rounders, lived a dramatically more privileged life than my own. Most of them attended private colleges on the East Coast. Some drove European sports cars into San Diego on their days off. The guys dressed in Goodwill clothes—jeans with holes and thin cotton button-down shirts, the kind favored by Mexican laborers—too tight and too worn. The women wore long woven smocks, generically ethnic, and patchouli oil. Everyone wore *huaraches*. When I explained it to my mother, she shrugged.

"A silver spoon and a paper plate," she said, as if this were normal, acceptable behavior. Inauthenticity, after all, is not a crime.

Midweek, some of the year-rounders stayed south of the border in a modest ranch-style home. They hauled water from a community well and used an outhouse and bought Coronas at the corner market by the case, then returned the empties for their deposits. They seemed happy. Their comfort zones were clearly broader than my own. They would have been as comfortable in a business suit, say, or sailing in the Mediterranean, as they were in a suburban Tijuana rambler, and I held it against them.

There was another volunteer, an acquaintance of mine from Eugene, at Los Niños. On our days off, she and I went to visit my family in Riverside to eat hamburgers and shop at Kmart. Getting back to our roots, we called it, while we ridiculed those pseudo-hippie coworkers—the one I worked with most often was planning an aerobics class for the teenaged girls at an orphanage. Aerobics for girls who would almost certainly be prostitutes in a matter of months? I was skeptical, and I admitted that I was thinking about quitting Los Niños.

"Why don't you teach swimming lessons?"

True, we took kids from various orphanages to public swimming pools once a week anyway. It was my favorite part of the job, if I had one.

"That's crazy," I said.

"No crazier than aerobics," she said.

"For America! Do it for America!" yells an immense woman, a new arrival. The woman circulates an oversized *turista* sombrero collecting money.

"This preacher says we don't got enough money to pay him. We gotta pay the man. This is America!"

Crumpled bills pile high. The Argus is packed as never before. I dig in my pocket for loose change to toss in the hat. Music scratches through the speakers, "La Bamba" yet again, and now everyone dances. A calloused hand slips into mine.

"What's your name?" I ask, leaning toward my partner. Before he can answer I am spinning away again, reaching for the closest hand in the crowd.

"Turn that thing off. I said turn it off. I'm about to get married here." The immense woman has left and returned in a white and yellow striped strapless tent of a sundress. She is barefoot and stands on a table covered with empty bottles that has been pushed aside to widen the dance floor. She hollers red-faced long after the jukebox has been silenced.

A gentlemanly drunk reaches out and escorts her down first to a chair then to the floor. Searchlights flicker and flee as the Harley roars into the hush.

The bridegroom appears in the doorway across the bar. He is lit from behind by the Coke machine and proudly attired in an elegant woven robe draped loosely over boxer shorts and a faded Mickey Mouse tank top. His sandals flap loudly over giggles and gasps. He shakes out an American flag and wraps it around himself, partially around his bride. They fuss over it like morning bedcovers.

Crazy Ray grunts and nods to the preacher.

"Do you, Ray ... ?"

Crazy Ray interrupts the preacher. "My name's not Ray," he says. "It's Crazy Ray!" He shifts his weight to stand a little taller.

"Do you, Crazy Ray, take this woman ... ?"

He does. She does. He pulls a ring from the robe pocket and places it in her nose. She does the same for him. The room explodes with laughter and cheers. Champagne sprays the grimy ceiling and soaks my shirt. The jukebox sparks up again mid-song. The new bride accepts dollar dances and parades across the floor dragging stars and stripes behind her. Crazy Ray rocks on a tipped chair in the corner wearing a permanent half-grin. When she remembers to, the bride races to him dramatically for a peck on the cheek, then she returns to the business at hand. We dance, all of us, until dawn: a loose weave tapestry of strangers held together by a hair-thin thread of joy.

Eventually night unravels into day. I gaze out, sleepless, to watch exhaust rising through still desert air as the orphanage vans warm up for another day, then stare down into the accumulated dust between my bare toes. By mid-morning fifty-seven kids, none of whom can swim, grip the too-high concrete lip of the pool and kick furiously. I holler myself hoarse in limited Spanish, blinded by the splashing. The Red Cross would say that I am teaching those kids just enough to be dangerous, but their lives are plenty dangerous already, and in such hot sun cool water is a relief, and this kicking, this wild wind-milling of arms gives all of us a fleeting sense of purpose and no small measure of glee.

The American teenagers urge the smallest kids to line up at the diving board, and I tread water, egg-beater kicking and waiting for them to pounce, coaxing them away from the edge in a cooing motherly tone, as I backpedal. I let them submerge then yank them back to the surface. Most places, kids would cry. In Tijuana, to a one, the kids arise gasping and choking and laughing, and I hold them tightly to my hip and sidestroke to safety. God help me, it's all I know how to do.

Did Crazy Ray get married at the Argus? For real? I don't know. I don't want to know. I know it was, without rival, the best night—maybe the only good night—I had in my season on the border. Crazy Ray lived eccentrically but deliberately, and one night he drew some people together. What if it was grand hoax, a giant scam in the name of America? God knows, it was neither the first nor the last. What if it was the real thing, whatever that is? Either way, I had an awfully good time. A few years later, when I took my first real creative writing class, Crazy Ray's was the first story I wanted to write, though I didn't know why. Years passed, and I kept trying. I wanted to capture the magic, I think, to show how community, like love and home and patriotism, could be as fleeting as helicopter search lights, as comforting and annoying as the same song played six thousand times on a jukebox, real even when it's based on a deception, and how connections—spontaneous, unexpected, even ridiculous—are worth celebrating. Inauthenticity, after all, is not a crime.

❧

By late afternoon the next day, I am driving the fourteen-passenger van north with a dozen American high school kids. As we slowly approach the tiny booth at *la linea* I disengage the clutch to inch forward and a small boy races across in front of the van, a garish Virgin Mary under one arm, Bart Simpson under the other. I barely miss him.

When we reach the front of the line, the border patrol guy recognizes me, or at least this Los Niños van, painted with huge smiling children's faces on the side. He's going to have some fun.

"Sing the ABC song," he says.

"A,B,C … " I begin. I do not even look at him.

What will come next is anyone's guess, The Pledge of Allegiance maybe, or a quick American history quiz.

The border patrol guy grins and nods. "Pretty nice," he says. "Real nice." He leans his head past me, so close I can smell his body odor and his chewing gum. Big Red.

"Place of birth?" he asks.

"U.S.," the teenagers mumble in turn, as they've been briefed to do, ad nauseum, for two days.

The teenagers have removed their sunglasses—also part of the briefing—and in the rear view mirror, they look, for once, small and a little scared.

"OK, OK," the border patrol guy says, waving us past, safely into the U.S. again.

I gaze up at the gigantic American flag, too heavy to rise in the wind, and I accelerate with traffic.

As soon as we pull away, the kids are in hysterics.

"Sing it again," they say. "Sing the ABC's again."

"ABC," I begin, and the teenagers join in and together we sing loud as we exit the interstate and speed east, our backs to the setting sun.

Sand-calloused Spaces

I'm sitting at Spanish Bottom, a wide sandy swath of beach beside the Colorado not far south of the confluence with the Green, trying to gauge the girth of the river. The muddy water—a splash of cream in dark coffee—flows deftly, competing currents plaiting like easy brushstrokes. A couple hundred yards across? A quarter mile? A half? I am no good at this. Better to be on the safe side. I unroll the blue insulated sleeping pad from my backpack, peel off my boots and socks, put on a pair of battered tennies packed for this occasion, and head upstream. I walk for half an hour, then enter the water. I'm thinking two things: that the currents will not be terribly strong and that the sleeping pad will work as a flotation device, like a super floppy surfboard, so that I can kick my way across leisurely with my head up. Right away, I see that I am wrong, wrong, wrong. The currents are plenty strong, and to make any progress at all, I will need full use of my arms. In a supreme act of faith and have-no-choice, I let go the pad, submerge my face, and begin to sprint. When I come up to breathe, I can see the blue pad floating away at remarkable speed, headed for Cataract Rapids—so close that I imagine I can see the pad undulating over the first early ripples—then to Lake Powell, and if it weren't for Glen Canyon Dam, right on downstream through the Grand Canyon. Next stop Vegas! I'm trying not to think about that.

40

Shortly after graduation, while lifeguarding full-time and mulling over options for the future, I'd torn a recruiter postcard off a university bulletin board, this one to volunteer in the national parks. I'd applied at Zion and the Grand Canyon, places I'd visited as a kid, but since the application required three choices I'd penciled in Canyonlands because the name sounded good and because the job requirements, including the willingness to hike in the heat and the ability to drive a stick shift, seemed pretty manageable.

The past months had left me in a funk. Nothing had gone particularly wrong. I'd enjoyed my last year of college. I'd spent time with good friends and graduated with good grades. Everyday life was not the problem. Not as far as I could tell. The big picture was the problem. Eight years of Reagan and one disconcerting summer working for Los Niños had left my idealism in tatters at twenty-two. I'd taken a political science course one quarter called "Crisis in Central America," taught by a too-angry professor who showed up in a more-than-usually shuddering rage one morning and explained the sketchy early details of a story that had just been reported on NPR—that U.S. officials had sold weapons to Iranian terrorists in exchange for the release of hostages and funneled the profits to Nicaraguan terrorists—and the entire class thought he had finally, completely, lost his mind. Later that day, we found out he'd been right. When it came to human interaction, it seemed, the worst was always possible, and the sheer complicatedness left me feeling awash in murky waters, floundering. On the dog-eared inside cover of my favorite novel, Marilynne Robinson's *Housekeeping,* I'd copied a section of dialogue where concerned townsfolk discuss the narrator, an awkward quiet girl: *One of them said, "Well, she seems so sad." And Sylvie replied, "Well, she is sad." Silence. "She should be sad." She laughed. "I don't mean she should be, but, you know, who wouldn't be?"* I'd reread the ballpoint scrawl, my inscription to myself, over and over during those months, and it felt right, like permission. Like the truth.

I arrived at Canyonlands after dark, threw my sleeping bag in the sand, and from the moment I awoke in that piercing desert emptiness, solitude cleared my mind like a clean damp cloth across a smeary slate. I realized, for one thing, that my own comfort zone was, apparently, turned inside out: things other people might consider hardships—idleness, silence, space— brought me relief, exhilaration even, while the so-called real world wore me thin. If I saw this as a peculiar fault, nothing to be proud of, I was at least glad to come clean. Behind the doublewide trailer I shared with a couple of roommates rose sandstone knobs that gripped tennis shoe soles even on unlikely steep pitches. In ten or fifteen long strides, you could sit alone with a long novel or a Dear Jane letter from yet another short-term boyfriend and let the unrest settle and churn, then dissipate into thin air. I felt saved, guiltily so, from the eternal thinking on injustice, the kind I caused and the kind I could do nothing about, saved from what I saw as the materialistic obscenity of American culture, of urban culture, the jerking and roiling of humans with humans. Saved also, it's worth mentioning, from finding a real job.

I know. I know. I should have thought about a career earlier— when I started college, say—but I'd assumed I'd join the Peace Corps, or short of that, I'd become a journalist, the *National Geographic* variety, savvy and smart with stylish eyewear and heavy camera equipment slung over one shoulder. Except that I was not savvy; I didn't take pictures; I didn't even wear glasses. More to the point, I didn't like asking people questions. I was starting to have trouble picturing a job other than lifeguarding that I might actually like when in Canyonlands—*voila!*—here it was!

My job as a Student Conversation Association volunteer was a plum. Half the time, I staffed the desk in the mobile trailer visitor center: selling books, giving directions, issuing permits. The other half of the time, I patrolled the backcountry: a fancy way of saying that I wore a uniform and walked all day. I stayed on the hard-beaten trails marked by rock cairns so as not to disturb the cryptogamic soil, a black crust coating the red sand. "Cryptogamic," the rangers had told us upon arrival, means "secret marriage" in Greek, and the soil was a fragile combination of fungus and algae that propagate by spores. We were to avoid stepping on it at all costs. The marriage, such as it was, seemed more tenacious than tenuous—you could look out at the red sand and see the pocks and hillocks of black cryptogamic soil everywhere—and it delighted me to think of it thriving in that dry land. Humans, it seemed, did not hold the sole lease on community.

As I patrolled, I'd meet the occasional visitor, check a permit, say, or give a little rattlesnake advice—leave them alone!—and move along. On the hottest days of summer, I worked a split shift. I walked from dawn to mid-morning, then hunkered in the shade of rock overhangs, cave-like and cool, that nearly always turned out to have pictographs on the walls, ancient graffiti, handprints or stick figures, human and animal. Eight hundred years old or older. What the pictographs meant nobody knew. What they meant didn't matter. What they meant was that I was not the first to seek shelter there, and in that simple knowledge, I was comforted.

I had felt a similar stirring the previous summer when I'd attended Mass in Mexico City in the grand Spanish cathedral built right on top of Aztec sacrificial altars. In church I'd always felt connected to others—to my long-dead ancestors and to strangers sitting beside me in the pews—by the search for meaning. In Mexico City, the cadences of the familiar prayers soothed me, as they had before, but there was more to it. Instead of the angry-professor outrage I knew I was supposed to feel about the conquest of one culture by another, I felt some stronger pull, a seduction, as if the place itself—this former island in a lake, thick-aired and abuzz with the threat of thunderstorms rolling off the distant mountains—held power greater than the Aztecs with their bloody sacrifices or the Spaniards with their bloody wars or American tourists like me with our faithless blundering. I'd felt less alone in that cathedral than anywhere else in Mexico, and I felt less alone on those sandstone cliffs in Canyonlands than I had in months. Go figure. I sat in silence through the midday heat, dozed occasionally, and soaked in the mysterious ancient presence until late in the afternoon when I'd walk again.

One day I heard a whistle ahead on the trail, a distinctly human whistle, evidence, I feared, that some hikers had brought along their dog—illegal on park trails. I moved toward the whistle, cowering at the prospect of having to give a scolding but feeling as though I owed the National Park Service this much. Another whistle. I approached a couple sitting on the canyon lip, their bare legs dangling over a dry sandy wash, thirty feet below. No dog to be seen.

The man rose to his feet as I approached and spoke in halting English, gesturing outward over the rock edge.

"We are from Germany," he explained. "We have never been anywhere so silent."

The woman with him nodded energetically and mimed an exaggerated expression of wonder. He whistled again, more quietly this time, and the three of us listened to the whistle slip away, echo faintly between low canyon walls, and head off to the Henry Mountains, a hundred miles beyond, hazy blips on the horizon. I nodded at the couple and smiled before leaving, but I said nothing. I didn't need to. I'd had conversations that lasted hours in which less was said.

Another day I ran into a father and his teenaged son who had driven a grueling twelve miles on a jeep trail to take photographs at twilight. They clearly meant to camp illegally, but I did not have the heart to tell them to leave. I made what meager small talk I could muster, and then we stood together in silence watching the sunset. Then I left. A year later I received a package from them forwarded by administrative staff at Canyonlands headquarters. In it were several black and white prints, the startling white edges of the canyons defined with such aesthetic clarity as to belie the labyrinthine reality, photos I've kept ever since as reminders of the beauty, and reminders, too, of the startling white-edged lesson I was learning amongst the canyons: that solitude, for those who shared the affinity for it, could breed companionability.

Two roommates shared my trailer with me, and after re-reading *Desert Solitaire*, I realized we had a pretty cushy deal: three bedrooms, two baths, and one glorious air conditioning wall unit. Ann was my age, fresh out of a college in Connecticut that she would not name. She had been a river guide for several summers, and she'd been a birder since childhood. She was capable, enthusiastic, and humble. Was it Yale? I asked. It was, of course, Yale. Judy was a veteran Park Service seasonal who suffered from eternal headaches, godawful headaches that she suspected stemmed from a swim she once took in a cow pond. Brain parasite, she said. Egads! we thought. Please try to keep quiet, she said. Ann and I did try, but sometimes, when we returned from our long days alone, our exuberance was too much. We listened to Joni Mitchell—*Ladies of the Canyon*—and we talked about books and boys, and mostly we prepared food:

fat-free soups and whole-grain muffins, and sour runny yogurt cultured in a six-pack Igloo cooler wrapped in dishtowels. To top it off, the rangers who had lived there in the spring had planted a garden, and deeded it to us when they left for the season, a boon at harvest time. Right out the front door, we had fresh peppers and eggplants and corn, too, and a tall willowy reddish plant that was remarkably prolific. Amaranth, someone told us, and we could not have been more excited if it had been the goose that laid golden eggs. Amaranth! Of course! We harvested the seed, winnowed the husks, and baked it into bread, basking in our good fortune. Afterwards, we retreated into our own separate silent worlds, into our bedrooms to read or out into the desert to walk, to refuel like junkies.

On my days off, I backpacked into the desert, or I saved my food stipend for gas money to drive to Telluride or to Flagstaff, long drives on two-lane roads across wide uninhabited spaces—Monument Valley, the Uncompahgre Plateau—and slept beside water wherever I could. I was seduced by water, comforted by the gently meandering muddy creeks tucked amongst red rocks, and of course, the Colorado. I often patrolled overlooks, but to actually reach the river, to shed your clothes and venture amidst the tamarisks, you'd have to either hike nine miles one way or drive to Moab, which I did often. I swam in the river and camped out beside it, and one Sunday I attended the Catholic church in town, just stood there among the faithful, my hair greasy with bug repellent from a gnatty night by the river, expecting to feel either repentant or exultant. Feeling neither was no small relief, like visiting an old boyfriend only to discover: I guess I'm done with that. I'd be searching for meaning elsewhere. I bought my groceries, boxed them with dry ice, and drove the eighty miles back home, descending toward the purple horizon, rising and dropping, rattling over cattle guards, watching the silhouetted knobs and formations against the darkening sky, feeling my heart grow large—not swelling, no, nothing so temporary or watery—but growing strong, sinewy even, as if it had finally found proper nourishment.

If the desert was less close and reassuring than the Northwest woods, it also felt roomier, infused with possibility. Patience grew easy as amaranth. (Even Judy's. Can you *please* keep it down? she asked nicely again and again and again.) Conversations moved slowly, punctuated by long lapses. I could feel myself adapting to sparseness, shedding layers like skin, even spending precious money to buy lightweight hikers, trading in my heavy leather waterproof stompers, the only boots I'd ever owned, for breathability. Monsoons arrived with the fall, and flash floods stampeded dry creek beds. Pine nuts ripened inside pinyon cones, and when I came home from patrolling, telltale pitch coated my fingers and my lips. Mule deer migrated down from the nearby mountains and grazed on Indian rice grass and Mormon Tea. I wore a T-shirt and shorts long into October, and my skin darkened, and my hair turned brittle blond in the sun, and sand calloused the spaces between my toes.

On one of my last trips to town before my volunteer season came to an end, I passed a coin-op newspaper stand outside a local diner and glanced at the headlines for the first time since my arrival in the desert. I had been aware of being out of touch with the real world; I'd reveled in it. Now *USA Today* taunted me. It was the first time I'd ever seen color photos in a newspaper, and I recoiled from the gaudiness, the large-font headline, assuming it must signal, yet again, something horrific. I wanted no part of it. But I was curious. Shielding the glass with one hand from the mid-afternoon glare, I bent closer and saw that the photos were of the Berlin Wall being torn down, and I thought for a moment that it was someone's idea of a joke, a terrible joke, before I realized that the unthinkable had indeed occurred. Not the squalid Iran/Contra, divide-and-conquer variety. But the precise opposite. I dug in my pockets for two quarters and plunked them in. Anything, it seemed, was possible.

Even swimming the Colorado River. In the center of Canyonlands, the Green river and the Colorado meet in a sprawling, listing Y that marks the district boundaries of the national park: the north district, the Island in the Sky, sits nestled in the V; the Needles, where I worked, is on the southeast flank; and the truly remote Maze district lies to the west across the stem, the wide muddy newly merged Colorado. To reach the Maze, you had either to drive several hundred miles, then drive further on treacherous four-wheel-drive roads, or you had to cross the river. I didn't own a four-wheel drive. No one had told me that it would be unwise to try to swim. No one had told me I couldn't. Later it would seem like a dangerous, nearly impossible, feat. Later yet it would seem like something to be proud of. Right then, I just knew, for once, what I wanted: I wanted to see the Maze.

I shouldered my pack and hiked the nine miles. It was mostly downhill, and it was too early in the day, too late in the season, to be genuinely hot, and I was in good shape. And the swim too, after the initial shock and the loss of the blue pad, was not so bad. Cataract Rapids might rival the Grand Canyon's in spring, just like the tourist brochures say, but in October the river runs lower and slower, and I felt strong and unfettered by doubts. Stroke stroke stroke, breathe right. Stroke, stroke, stroke, breathe left. I climbed out of the river exuberant over my success—the Maze!—before I realized that, since I couldn't swim with a bottle or a water filter, I did not have enough drinking water to stay long. So I explored a bit, then walked upstream for half an hour, a harder task on this craggier side of the river, and swam back across.

❨

On the return swim, shadows have begun to stretch across the water, and it feels less menacing, refreshing even, to be stroking so hard back to safety. The current feels not unlike a rip tide, terrifying and enticing—inevitable as my real-world future—but I swim hard across, fighting it, knowing it is, for me, dangerous. When I lift my head from the water to see where I am, I see that I have swum too hard, that I will reach shore too far upstream and will have to crash back through the tamarisks, so I sidestroke back out into the current, and ride it for awhile, watching the towering canyon walls against the rich blue sky. When I see my camp, I stroke hard once, twice, three times and rise up again onto the beach.

Later, as evening descends, a group of women on a paid river trip settles in to camp directly across the river. I filter river water through my bandanna and boil it to drink. In the narrow canyon I lie down in sand under a stripe of starlight trimmed by the dark. From across the river, middle-aged women's voices rise and fall. Their laughter is a little too loud, but I don't mind. They've noticed me, a young woman alone, and they're impressed—I can hear them say as much—and a tiny grain of pride is growing pearl-like within my shell. Someday, I think, this shell will shatter open, and it will feel precisely as fine as this: sleeping alone in sand under the stars and awakening to the shock of a jack rabbit stealing out from under bitterbrush.

The Fall Line

The slope drops steeply, snow-sodden, and out of view. My ski tips hover suspended in air for a moment before—with a sharp swoop of caught-breath—I slide over the edge. Telemarking, for real! I descend, genuflecting once, rising in exultation, one foot sluicing beside the next, then down on the other knee, leaning down the fall line. Down then up in the sun. Nothing to it! Except that I am not actually skiing. I am driving fast on Interstate 10 across the Mojave, sun-blinded. And perhaps I am love-blinded. Though I don't know it. I can't yet imagine that possibility. But I can imagine myself telemarking—the ancient Norwegian technique for checking downhill speed on cross-country skis—quite keenly. Truth is, I can't ski to save my life.

When I left Stehekin for the first time that November, a year after my stint in Canyonlands, I expected a shock. Veteran seasonals—those who came to the valley each spring to work for the National Park Service and left each fall—nodded knowingly, with exaggerated wistfulness, as they told me how hard it would be to readjust to driving on interstates, to talking on telephones. Just scanning the aisles of a grocery store, they said, would amount to sensory overload: all those brands of cereal to choose from! I found the transition easy. Too easy. Just step on the gas and go. Pull out a credit card and sign. I landed back in Riverside, California—where I'd grown up—to visit my mother and quickly discovered that nothing much had changed

during my six months uplake, least of all me. I found that stark
reality a lot more shocking than a cereal aisle. And a whole lot
more depressing.

I hung around my mother's empty house, reading the local
paper and avoiding the television like the plague, as if watching
mid-morning *I Love Lucy* reruns might be the final fatal blow to
my sense of self. Sunlight exposed the kitchen table littered with
junk mail and my empty crusting cereal bowl. Dogs barked a
twenty-minute prelude as the mailman approached, and I waited
for his footsteps, then I leaped.

This is how I spent most of my time: I wrote long letters
to Laurie, my roommate from summer, and she wrote back.
I addressed the envelopes fastidiously, decorating them with
colored pencils—my return address palm trees, hers firs—like
a child with a new pen pal, like a much younger girl. We'd met
back in the spring. Tan and blond, in a tattered hooded University
of Washington sweatshirt, Laurie seemed impossibly cool,
certainly too cool to be my friend—she wore RayBans, she drove
a Toyota Tercel with a sun roof—but she was friendly enough
and generous to boot. She opened a bottle of Gewürztraminer,
sweet dessert wine in a slender bottle, the kind of extravagance
I'd never have sprung for, and she poured two mugs. We talked
about our pasts and our outdoorsy adventures, though hers
clearly outstripped mine: she had been a ranger in a fire lookout
in Glacier Peak Wilderness and a ski bum at Mt. Bachelor, a
laborer at Mt. Rainier, a firefighter in Yellowstone, and most
recently, a tree-planter in the Ochocos. Me, I'd been a lifeguard
in Eugene. Mostly, like girls anywhere, we talked about boys. I'd
recently navigated a series of comically ill-fated entanglements,
while Laurie dangled several prospects across the West, whose
names were similar enough to be a little confusing: Mike, Mick,
two Scotts. We figured we'd get along famously, and we did, all
through a glorious summer and into the fall, with no designs for

the future, none at all, until finally we hatched a plan. We'd rent a cabin with our friend, Larry, from trail crew, and we'd spend the winter in Stehekin.

Now, in California, I waited, anxiously suspended.

One night I attended a bachelorette party at a bar in Hollywood where the drinks came in neon colors and the other women wore tight mini skirts, and I wore blue jeans with a sweater. Bar patrons danced to the English Beat in front of mirrors while a surfer crouched in the half-pipe of a crashing wave on a dozen TV screens at once, and I felt sick with longing watching him, though I couldn't surf anymore than I could ski. On the ride home, all of us nauseous, we had the requisite girl talk—sex, sex, sex—and it was the first time in my life I'd participated in girl talk. As it turned out, it would be the last.

The next morning I drove ten hours to Tucson to visit a friend of a friend who had been a well-known womanizer back in college, a guy I'd met once at a wedding. I swiped my sister's car—the "Goes-Eighty-Audi," she called it—for the trip and sped east across the desert in time to knock on his front door and drag him out for dinner. I leaned in close and laughed loud, but no dice: he didn't return my awkward flirtations. I slept on his hideaway, and in the early morning, stopped at REI to buy telemark skis, my first pair ever. Then I raced home, driving the Audi too fast, RPMs flickering at the high end of the gauge.

That's when I dreamed of skiing. I dreamed for hours as the wide Mojave shimmered yellow and the traffic shushed past. I dreamed for so long that, by the time I pulled into my mother's driveway, my quadriceps ached, and I was elated. How astonishingly easy it is, I thought, to stay on your feet! And I was right. Just not about the skiing.

Back at my mother's house, letters from both Laurie and Larry awaited. Larry reported that he'd spent November splitting and stacking six cords of firewood that he had bought for fifty bucks from a shady local known as Murky who was moving out of town. Larry would be leaving Stehekin soon, too, he said, to visit his family in Connecticut for the holidays, but he was excited about returning for the winter. Winter in paradise, he called it. Laurie's news was less encouraging. She was nursing a nasty stomach bug—later it would be diagnosed as giardia—and nurturing a flailing relationship with an engineer boyfriend. She said she'd join the boyfriend on an after-Christmas ski trip to Lake Tahoe, then come to Stehekin after that. So it was set. In a month, I'd be the first to return to paradise, alone, to the house Larry rented from friends for a ridiculously low rate, a four-bedroom cabin with vaulted ceilings and a huge woodstove fashioned from an oil barrel. I could hardly wait. I could almost hear kindling crackle and catch to steal the edge of chill from the cabin dawn. I could see mountains pasted white against cloudless blue—just like an REI catalog cover!—and I could feel the fresh powder surrender so softly under those new skis in the garage.

I raced north on 1-5 for three days, took a hard right at Seattle, and drove over the mountains to Chelan. Then I boarded the boat for the four-hour ride. In Stehekin, I showed up travel-weary and deeply chilled. I tromped a hundred yards through wet snow to reach the cabin, stepped into the woodshed, and looked around me. Aghast.

When I was in college I'd lived in a house where we'd heated with wood, rationed our wood actually, obsessively, shivering under electric blankets, studying at the library. I knew very well what a cord of firewood was. Four feet wide, four feet deep, eight feet long. Stacked tidily, a single cord of wood looks like two large refrigerators lying on their sides. This measly pile was not even that, and whether it was Murky's fault—the crook selling half a cord as six—or Larry's ignorance, the upshot was that we did not have enough wood. Not even close. The next week the temperature dropped to single digits and the pipes under the house froze solid. I crawled under the house with a hair dryer to thaw them, and I waited for Larry to arrive.

"Where are the six cords of wood?" I asked when he did.

"These are them," he said.

I didn't argue. The truth would become apparent soon enough, and tension, in paradise, would mount. Larry had a passion for obscure Chicago bluesmen whose music I loathed. I preferred Jim Croce, earnest and unabashed, and when, later in the winter, my cassette tangled and knotted in the tape player, Larry nearly wept with joy. A stray cat frequented the porch, and when Larry fed it, I was furious.

"Get rid of it," I cried.

"How?" Larry asked. He laughed.

I wished, right then, with all my might, for Laurie. Her contagious buoyancy would solve the household problems in a snap. More importantly, she'd be able to help us get more wood. We needed willing labor, plenty of it, and soon. But her latest letter reported that the giardia had taken a toll and that it would be another couple weeks before she could make the trip uplake. We, in the icy cold house, could not wait that long.

The search for firewood had to begin. We heard about a snow-buried log along the lakeshore, and went to cut it at boat time, the middle-of-the-day hour when nearly everyone in town drove the one landlocked road to pick up their mail. Clouds hung low in an inversion, trapping cold air and woodsmoke. Not knowing the first rule of chainsaws—never borrow one!—we borrowed a chainsaw from Phil Garfoot, our trail crew boss, and dulled the chain to nubbins. Locals drove past us slowly, nodding in greeting, hiding their smirks. What's worse, that log didn't begin to solve our problem. We filled one corner of the woodshed, and within a week it was empty again. We knew cutting a live tree would do us no good, since it would need at least a year to dry out, so we were at a loss, until Phil showed up to help.

Before he'd settled down to have a family, Phil had traveled the world as a merchant marine. Now he was a trails worker— in his fifties and *still* a trails worker! On his days off, he shoed horses for the local packer. At home, he wore Birkenstocks and collected coffee-table books of the great American illustrators, a profession he had once hoped to pursue, and other books too, walls of books by hard-living northern Europeans that he resembled not a little: Joseph Conrad, Knut Hamsen, Thor Heyerdahl. He told us about another tree that the owner of the house we were renting had felled a few years earlier. The cut tree, he said, had hung up between two live standing trees, and there it remained, suspended, a boon for us, especially since the owner had a firewood permit for it, an out-of-date permit, granted, but a permit nonetheless. Phil even offered to cut the tree because neither Larry nor I was any good with a chainsaw—to prove it we'd ruined that perfectly good chain only a week before—and because cutting a hung-up tree in a snowstorm near power lines would be no easy feat. He perched on a ladder in coveralls, running a chainsaw over his head with one hand and gripping icy ladder rungs with the other.

While Phil sawed, out of nowhere, the district ranger appeared. I thought he might lend a hand. He was, after all, a law enforcement ranger in a valley that hadn't seen a felony in thirty years, and he was most assuredly on the clock. His green-and-gray polyester uniform strained at the buttons.

"Howdy," he said. "What're you up to?"

I explained the permit and Murky's six-cord trick and the fact that we were out of firewood and, really, very cold, and then went about loading the pickup we'd borrowed as the snowflakes grew larger, the size of quarters, then cottonwood leaves.

The ranger just stood there watching. Then he left.

The tree itself was not much good, punky and ant-gnawed, the kind of wood that would burn like balsa, not enough heat per log to last one verse of "Time in a Bottle." But heat nonetheless. We loaded the too-light rounds into the truck and drove them closer to the house. From there, we dragged the wood on sleds a hundred yards or so, several trips' worth, and stacked it, finally, in the woodshed before dark. Almost a full cord. Success! Phil went home. Larry went to work in a neighbor's woodshop. I collapsed on the couch and pulled a sleeping bag over me to keep warm. Everything, it seemed, might turn out OK. This tree was a start.

I gazed out the picture windows. Our cabin sat in one of the few clearings in the fir-clogged valley, a fairway from a golf course planned in the 1920s that never came to fruition. The clearing allowed moonlight to shine hazily through the windows like lamplight seeping from a closed-door room. Like possibility. Except that the moon couldn't be out: storm clouds obscured the sky. The light, I realized, must be headlights reflecting off the snow from afar and brightening the underside of the leafless yellow-stemmed willow in the yard. Larry hadn't taken the truck so I couldn't imagine who it could be. I heard boots stomp onto the porch, then a loud knock, and I dragged myself off the couch to open the door and let the last dregs of heat drain into the night.

There stood the ranger.

"You'll have to return the stolen property," he said.

What stolen property? For a moment I didn't know. Then, all of a weary sudden, I did know.

"We had a permit," I said.

"That permit was out of date and you know it. If you return the wood to the park maintenance shop, I won't write tickets," he said.

"Oh, come on," I said. I was tired and cold and had, so far as I could tell, not a thing to lose in the world. "You can't be serious. What do you want from me?"

"Heads are gonna roll."

He'd found this line, I was pretty sure, in a detective novel. I stared at him and, after a stony silence, he left.

When Larry returned, I told him about the ultimatum.

"No way am I moving that wood again," I said.

"We have to," Larry pleaded. "My trail-crew job depends on it."

I couldn't believe it. His job-at-risk excuse held no water. Phil was Larry's boss, not the ranger, and besides, Larry had told us often how he planned to apply to grad school and put manual labor behind him. His nonchalance had, in fact, helped me avoid worry about my own re-hire prospects. The stray cat mewed at my feet and rubbed against my wool pants, and I wished again that Laurie were there to take my side, but I knew that when it came down to it, she wouldn't. I knew that, without a thought, always—no matter how flimsy the excuse—Laurie would side with whoever was most vulnerable, or in this case, desperate. The stray cat, definitely. Larry, probably.

"OK," I said. "OK."

Larry and I put on headlamps and trudged into the woodshed to fill the sleds again, over and over, and drag the newly split firewood back across the yard and through the plowed parking area, sleds scraping, to the maintenance shop where we unloaded the wood and re-stacked it as requested. We did not finish until well after midnight, when we stumbled home to bed, silent and spent.

A week later, Laurie arrived at last, with drugs for her gut and a quiver of skis. Both Larry and I met her at the boat landing.

"How was Tahoe?" I asked.

"A disaster," she said, hugging me. "I couldn't eat, much less ski."

"That's too bad," I said.

"And you," she said to Larry. "How could you?"

The very question I'd avoided asking all along.

"How could I what?"

"How could you screw up the firewood so bad?"

Larry laughed weakly and shrugged. It was the first time I'd ever seen him speechless and the first time, too, that I considered that maybe Larry did feel bad about his mistake.

"You dingaling," Laurie said. And they hugged, too.

The three of us settled into an agreeably decadent truce. We ate pancakes with chocolate chips for dinner. We drank Schmidt's beer and hot chocolate mixed together in a foamy malt and pretended it tasted good. We took the splitting maul and chipped ice off the five-gallon buckets of apple cider we had pressed in the fall and melted it in a saucepan on the electric stove, since the woodstove was never warm enough to melt ice. Sometimes, after we faded to bed, we heard the slapping of beaver tails on the mill pond behind the cabin. Usually we heard only the din of snow sliding off the roof and the more menacing thunder of distant avalanches. Then we'd get up early and head for the hills.

With a couple of friends, Bob and Jonathan, avid skiers who never complained about the weather or the lousy snow conditions, we set out, leaving Larry, the non-skier, at home. Using headlamps, we slogged upwards for hours with climbing skins glued to the bottom of our skis to keep us from sliding back, taking turns breaking trail in the cakey snow. It was hard work, an immense amount of work, but I loved being out in the mountains, above the valley, looking across at the dark veins of trees fanning down from the peaks, broken only by the clean white gullies, avalanche chutes, sheer and narrow and numerous. The pre-Technicolor world was hypnotizing, entrancing. At the top, we stopped to remove our skins, and the guys talked Laurie into making the first tracks. She dropped down the fall line—the skier's sweet spot, the most direct path downhill, the way a ball would go if you rolled it—and the three of us stood agog. Laurie skied like she was doing an elaborate dance, carefree and utterly ecstatic. Watching her reminded me how easy it was. The fact that I tumbled most of the way down—that it was a comical version of my Mojave vision, the Mr. Magoo version, just this side of catastrophe—did not faze me one bit. I had imagined I could ski when I was in the desert, and I was twenty-three, high on the mountains, and deeply stubborn.

Laurie traveled one weekend to Seattle to put an end, she said, to business with the engineer, and she zipped off the next weekend to ski in Idaho with some tree-planter friends. She traveled often, sleeping in her Tercel, eating pickled herring on the run, scribbling on a notepad propped against the steering wheel on straight stretches of the interstate. Her "road journal," she called it. And I stayed home where the snow turned to rain, and the firewood pile dwindled again. When the avid skiers planned an overnight trip to a wall tent that another pal, Dave, had stashed four thousand feet up on McGregor Mountain, I packed right away, and met them pre-dawn at the trailhead. The guys promised that by the time we reached four thousand feet the syrupy rain would turn to pellety snow. But it did not. Rain continued to fall as we climbed for seven hours in heavy sopping snow, in heavy sopping clothes, gazing out through swirling clouds for rare glimpses of the mountains across the valley or the small frozen lake below. When at last we reached the tent site, we were soaked to the sweaty skin and very cold.

"Now, where's that tent?" one of the guys asked.

"Well," Dave said, "it's under that one big tree."

One big tree? One big tree? In a forest crammed tight with big trees, equally big trees, hundreds of them? I grew angry, then panicked. We unpacked our avalanche shovels and began shoveling madly under one tree then another, a dozen deep pits of snow, until darkness threatened, and even if we found the tent, it would take too much time to set it up. So we turned and skied down, or they skied and I stumbled. Part way down, we broke into a backcountry cabin and started a fire in the stove and slept hard in the suffocating steam of wet clothes drying on parachute cord.

Winter, I had to admit, was not turning out exactly the way I'd hoped. The REI catalog-cover version of paradise, all sun-streaked and powdery perfect, had not materialized. Nor had there been much in the way of cabin-in-the-woods serenity. Our cabin wasn't warm enough for hanging around, and when we did, some bluesman was always caterwauling that his woman done him wrong. The next day I arrived back home exhausted and opened the door with my shoulder, the weight of snow having shifted the jamb again, and entered. I'd expected the house to be empty—Larry spent most of his time at the neighbor's wood shop—but it was not.

"It's over," Laurie said.

"The engineer?"

She nodded.

In the cabin, the barrel stove sat atop a pedestal of rock for ease of loading—if we'd ever had any wood to load—and the carpet was brown and worn. Lamps in each corner of the big room provided the only light. That night Laurie was retelling the story of a trip to South America, and she pulled out her journal to look for a passage to make a point. Laurie flipped through the pages. She sat hunched cross-legged on the floor as daylight faded at three-thirty, and she read. I sat across the room and listened. The Schmidt cans emptied, and we didn't go for more. The tape player stopped, and we didn't put in another. The night grew dark, and Laurie scooted into a corner, closer to the light, farther from the fire, which had, anyway, long since gone out. And she just kept reading.

Not that reading to each other was anything new. On mail days, three days a week, Laurie and I would ski or bike to the boat landing and sit on the dock reading letters from distant friends aloud. News of the Gulf War permeated the letters, but we could not have cared less. War news, like petty injustice and the smoky inversion, floated heavily around us never close enough to snag. The so-called real world ceased to exist. On yet another ski trip, we had followed Bob and Jonathan half-way toward a high pass near the lake, carrying overnight gear, before giving up, letting the guys go on ahead, and setting up a tentless camp with garbage bags as bivvy sacks on the nose of a ridge. We stabbed our skis into the crust to pen us in, to keep us from slipping over the edge. Many hours of daylight remained and we spent them reading aloud to each other from a collection of short stories about unlikely backwoodsy characters. We took turns until it was too dark to make out the print as stars began to flicker close, a hundred million of them, and the temperature dropped, then dropped some more, and a tiny upturned fingernail snip of moon rose across the lake from behind a craggy ridge, and beamed bright, reflecting off the snow, putting off more light than should have been possible. The moon skirted the mountain peaks like a skiff over waves—never rising higher, never dropping lower—and we sat upright bundled in our sleeping bags, watching entranced, waiting for it to set. But it never did. The moon-boat just kept floating along the ridgeline.

"They're aliens!" Laurie announced. "They're coming to get us." And why not?

We jumped from our sleeping bags and waved our arms like castaways flagging a passing vessel, and we yelled with our hoarse lungs.

"Take us with you," we cried. "We're here."

Back in the cabin, Laurie finished reading the journal. She'd read about the deckhands who stole her friend's shoes while they slept on a banana barge on the Amazon, and about the pilot who fixed a Cessna with Pepsi cans so he could fly her and her friends out of the way of the Shining Path, and about her friend/boyfriend on the trip, how the relationship had not worked out, and how, finally, scared and sad she had been the entire time. She closed the journal shivering hard, as much from exposing so much of herself as from the cold. Even I knew that. But I did not know what to say. What is there to say? We climbed the stairs to the large bedroom we shared in silence. Laurie had the large double bed in the middle of the room, while I slept on a pad on the floor under a cozy dormer window because I preferred to see the sky. From under my layers of accumulated blankets, I could see a swath of unmasked stars—such a rare sight—and I could hear Laurie's teeth chattering. Any other time, I may have been cautious or prudent, I may have considered the consequences—what Laurie might think, for starters—but that winter I was accustomed to leaping first, and looking later.

I crawled out of my bed to lie on top of her bedcovers and try to warm her, and after a while I began to shiver, so when I went back to my nest on the floor, Laurie came to warm me. This time, finally, it only made sense for us both to get under the covers.

We lay spooned together, tense and perfectly still, and we held hands, our fingers cupped lightly, one in the other, like newly broken eggshells, and the adrenaline swoop in my chest felt like dropping down the fall line in my dream, delicious and nearly real as skiing the Mojave. Except that, right then, I knew this was not nearly real, but really real. What's more, I knew I'd always known. Slowly, in silence, we began to trace the icy cold tendons along the backs of our thumbs, and our movements were both tentative and sure, and the adrenaline rush softened, and warmth spread from the tingly piqued fingertips out through the whole of me, and—I could tell—the whole of Laurie, the whole lovely valley, and the wide universe, too. I could hear my own heart beat, strong and fast and loud, and I could hear the roof settling under snow weight, and I don't think I slept as we held hands, but instead, just kept falling, chest in my throat, the way you do in a dream where you know you will never ever hit bottom, because if you do, you will die.

The next morning, Larry tried to bring us coffee in bed, only to see us together and turn on his heels. Laurie and I rose, skipped breakfast, and skied in different directions. I didn't know where to go. Like my father's death, this unforeseen change knocked me entirely off balance like sliding, skis and poles flailing, through the heavy slop or somersaulting through the churning waves of an avalanche. I know. I know. Falling in love happens to everyone. But when you're in it, there's no way to know whether danger is imminent. Cliffs over the next rise? Rocks under the surface? The only choices are to try like hell to get up and keep going. Or to run away. Me, I ran to the boat landing.

A low bank of clouds, the omnipresent inversion, drew a stark line across the hills: whiteness above trees blurred nearly black. The lake lay impervious. Nothing to reflect. I stood stiff and over-bundled a few hundred feet apart from the crowd gathered to meet the ferry. The rush from the night before had turned to an ache and I told myself that maybe, like an infection that starts to itch, that might mean that soon the wound would heal and the feeling would disappear. That thought made the ache worse, made it sink deeper, knife-twisting in my gut like giardia, a condition that, if not treated, keeps coming back. I knew what the treatment for my ache would be—to stay with Laurie—and I knew, or at least told myself, that staying together was a no-go, an impossibility. For one thing, Laurie would never consider it.

If she did, that would be worse yet. Wouldn't it? I took off my wool cap to brush a few stray raindrops through my ponytail. Things could not possibly get more complicated.

Right then, the district ranger strode toward me in full uniform, Stetson perched too-high on his head, and handed me a ticket for cutting firewood illegally, a violation that carried a fifty-dollar fine. And even though I was angry, even though we'd done exactly as he'd demanded that night and returned the wood to the maintenance shop, even though fifty bucks was more than I'd had to my name in months, I took the damned thing and pocketed it. Fine. Fine. I did not have the time for this. He'd issue tickets eventually to Phil and Larry, too. Larry would decide to pay. Phil would vow to fight it Gary Cooper-style for all he was worth—a *High Noon* standoff on the horizon—in federal court in Spokane.

In the evening, back home, Laurie and I tried to pretend that nothing had changed. Larry put Elvis Costello in the tape deck, a generous neutral choice, and waited for an explanation that didn't yet exist. A couple of ninety-minute pleading loops later—*what's so funny about peace, love, and understanding?*—Larry gave up and went to his room. Laurie and I headed to our separate dormers. What to do, we had no idea. What *not* to do—sleep together—we knew that much. But it was no good. Sometime in the night one of us moved, and we spooned together silently and slept. We didn't know what we were getting into. We didn't talk about it. The following day we avoided each other all over again, and when I came home from skiing, an unexpected guest sat in the living room: the engineer boyfriend.

"Hi," I said.

He nodded. His bags, at his feet, were still packed. I could tell immediately that Laurie had already said something to him.

She had. She told him what we'd be telling people for the next several years by way of explanation: The house was cold! We held hands!

Then Laurie told him more. We think we are in love, she said to him, even though we had not yet said this to each other.

The boyfriend told her this: You have to give it a try. If you don't, you'll wonder forever. Your heart will never be open to anything else.

"He said we have to give it a try," Laurie said to me. We'd moved upstairs under the dormer to talk this out alone. "You and me." She had been crying, and now she was crying again. "What do you think?" she asked.

"I will if you will," I said.

The boyfriend left the next day. I tried to thank him, but choked instead—more crying, so much crying—and hugged him, and he was gone.

Larry presented each of us, Laurie and me, with identical hand-crafted letter boxes that he'd been working on all winter, the joints tight, the surface sanded smooth.

"Thank you," I said. But it wasn't enough. I hadn't heard the mewing stray cat in weeks, and Larry couldn't quite make eye contact. He shrugged.

"We'd better do something about the firewood," he said.

So we did. We bought a cord of apple wood from orchardists tearing out less-than-profitable trees and had it barged uplake, and the cabin, at last, was warm.

Come spring, I decided to join Phil in federal court. Why not? I knew we'd been foolish to go into the winter so unprepared, and I knew we'd technically broken the law. Still, the facts seemed so arbitrary, so obviously less important than the plain truth: we'd been cold, and we'd tried to get warm. Snow in Spokane was, by then, long gone. Outside the courthouse, cherry blossoms floated pink against cloud-spackled blue. Inside, we crowded close on wooden pews—Laurie, Phil, and I—while the district ranger and other federal officials sat on padded swivel chairs surrounding the judge on a carpeted podium, and we waited eight long hours for the case to be called. By the time Phil stood to read his notes, it was nearly four thirty, and the judge was short on patience. He interrupted Phil several times trying to get the facts straight—who works for who here?—before he got the gist and dismissed him with a wave of his hand.

"Does the young lady have anything to say?" he asked.

I came forward.

"Did the ranger say anything else to you that night?" the judge asked.

I cleared my throat. "He said, 'Heads are gonna roll,'" I said.

The judge raised one hand to stop me right there. He could not dismiss the charges, he explained, but he could reduce our fines to five bucks each. Ignorance, the judge implied, is not a crime. Petty meanness, on the other hand, is vile. He pounded the gavel and hurried us on our way. We stepped out of the courthouse, blinking, trying to adjust to the newness of the too-bright sun, of springtime newly arrived.

Winter was over. Life had begun.

It would be many years before I could telemark passably. It would be nearly as long before Laurie and I settled completely into our relationship, and longer yet before we settled in Stehekin and cut six cords of wood for ourselves. Nothing, it turned out, would ever be quite as easy as skiing the Mojave, but the desert dream stuck like muscle memory. Like courage. God knows we'd be needing it.

This, Jack London Reminded Me

Midwinter sunlight reflected yellow and glary from snowy peaks, so close, and up from the tops of clouds that grouted the spaces between them. On the three-sixty horizon, I could see hundreds of mountain peaks, like sails on the wind, and in the soft white curves of the basin below, I could see our day, as sunset neared, in dozens of long continuous S marks, the grace and pluck of movements—aggressive, tentative, jaunty, exuberant—captured in the squiggles skiers left. This winter view from Ten Mile Pass trumped any view I'd seen in summer by a long shot. In my memory it shines more brightly than the substantial misery that followed. Even now, so many years later, when I prefer to spend winter typing in a too-warm cabin in a gray-drenched forest, I'm glad to know the higher world exists: brilliant, incandescent, not so far off.

The trip had begun three days earlier when Bob ferried us across the river from his cabin to the trailhead in a wooden skiff he'd built himself. Besides being a skier, Bob was a boat builder and a mountain climber, a former army ranger with irrepressible energy and a five-month-old son at home. A month earlier he'd ice-climbed Rainbow Falls even as the temperature rose and pitons loosened like baby teeth, but Bob shrugged off the danger. Trips into the mountains fed his spirit. He'd go no matter what. If friends came along, all the better. This time he'd invited Jonathan and Tom, and he'd invited Laurie and me. Both excellent skiers, self-taught in these roadless mountains, where to practice going downhill you have to spend several hours slogging up, Jonathan and Tom knew what they were getting into. Laurie, who'd spent a couple of winters backcountry skiing in Central Oregon, probably knew what she was getting into, too. I didn't. Though it's hard to imagine that knowing would have changed much. We'd held hands for the first time only a week before. Nothing could be as scary as that. I'd go no matter what.

No matter, for example, that I'd only been snow camping twice before, once on entirely flat ground. Just packing for the four-day excursion proved a challenge. The trip required, at the very least, heavy army surplus wool pants, a heavy ragg wool sweater, and two heavy sleeping bags. When I swung the load from my right knee onto my back to try it out, my knees buckled. To top it off I'd borrowed a pair of skis. Faster skis, everyone insisted. As if that was a good thing. It's easy, with hindsight, to say that the trip taught me a lesson, precisely the lesson you're supposed to learn at twenty-three: that actions have consequences. But that's not half the story.

We crossed the river and shouldered our packs, then crossed a couple more mucky sidearm sloughs balancing on slick downed logs with our overfull packs, skis strapped to the sides and towering over our heads, and then, finally, we glued on climbing skins, stepped into our ski bindings, and headed up. The trail was steep at first, but I wasn't too concerned. I knew that once we hit a middling elevation things would level off. Besides, going up was my forte, the only direction where pure-guts-and-no-skill count for something. My thighs ached from the weight, and my lungs burned from cold, but I managed to stay in the middle of the group as we switchbacked single file up and around the broad nose of a ridge and into the narrow drainage where Devore Creek, gurgling several hundred feet below us, sounded too close and foreboding. When Bob grew tired out in front, he stepped aside to let Jonathan take over breaking trail, and when Jonathan stepped aside to let us by, with heavy ice build-up atop his moustache like Yeti, his alter ego, he grinned like mad. When it came to my turn, I lifted my ski high and lunged into the heavy snow, one foot then the next, making way for the others, doing my part.

By mid-morning, sure enough, we began to traverse instead of climb. And traversing might have been easier than climbing except for the avalanche chutes that bisected the trail at regular intervals. The weather was too cold and the snow too stable for us to worry about avalanches. That wasn't the problem. The problem was that the chutes were littered with huge ice balls—translucent blue, basketball-sized, and almost perfectly spherical—like so many decapitated snowmen. We'd step up to balance circus-style on one ski atop an ice ball, then maneuver the second ski around and amongst the other balls to meet the first, then step to the next ball. It took twenty minutes to cover thirty feet. We'd cross one chute, ski another few hundred yards, then cross another, for most of the afternoon—how many chutes could there possibly be? A dozen? Two dozen? More?—until, finally, as the day grew darker, we veered into the woods and continued to climb. As we moved together, higher and higher, toward the peaks, the snow grew lighter, but my legs grew wobbly, my breath wheezy. The others seemed unfazed. They moved ahead, and after a while, after my heroic stab at the early switchbacks, I no longer broke trail. The other four each took a turn, but when I reached the front of the line, Bob charged ahead to take an extra turn. Eventually I fell behind completely. If it was humiliating, it was also exhilarating to be on my own at last in the silent snowy woods—like a Jack London character—high on endorphins and warm with exertion, so many miles from so-called civilization.

That first night, we set up camp and boiled soup. Soon sweat-soaked skin chilled under layers of wool and down. Conversations stalled. Shivering ensued. After watching tiny zipper-mounted thermometers dip toward zero, we began to gather armloads of kindling in the dark. Beneath the pillows of snow perched on higher limbs, dry twigs snapped. We crammed them around a smallish dead tree poking out of the snow and struck a match. The fire caught. As it burned, the five of us sat with our legs dangling into the pit it made, sinking as our snow benches melted, and watching the fire tower higher and higher above. We laughed and sipped hot chocolate, and the camaraderie felt every bit as illusionary as the flaming snag rising into the star-specked sky.

Illusionary, I say, because I was pretty sure I'd never see those guys again. The end of winter hastened near, and whatever I ended up doing, I figured I wouldn't be staying. Who could have guessed, on that star-blinded night, that a decade later Bob and Jonathan would be the ones to help Laurie and me build a house, or that in the middle of those grubby construction marathons, I'd change into clean clothes to go tutor Tom's daughter, a home-schooled tenth grader? At the time, it seemed ridiculously unlikely.

The next afternoon we arrived at the pass. It had become obvious because of conditions, and maybe because of my own lousy physical condition—I'd been lagging far behind the others—that we wouldn't be making the twenty-five-mile loop we'd planned, but would just be skiing from the pass for a day before turning around. That evening, without a word to any of us, Tom headed up a steep slope and began to creep around the side of the mountain to see what he could see of the terrain we wouldn't reach. We sat in silence and watched as Tom broke trail alone, a solitary dark silhouette, like a dust speck on a lens, against a wall of white. At the ridgeline, he stopped. How he'd get back down, I couldn't imagine; the slope was cliffy in spots. When he turned around in the last dusky snatch of daylight, he moved slowly down the slope in wide careful swooping turns, leaving graceful S's across the sharp switchback Z's of his ascent. He descended so effortlessly that I could imagine him whistling under his breath. I watched in awe. I admired the easy balance he'd found in life as on skis, and I wondered if I could ever find it myself. When he returned to camp, he dug into his pack and pulled out a six-pack of beer. He passed them out, and the silence snapped as we sat by headlamp cradling dark beer in mittens, miles from any human soul, laughing and whooping it up. We'd made it! And tomorrow we'd ski.

Or most of us would. The next day, when everyone took telemark runs down from the pass, I gamely followed along, tumbling down the hill, then rolling around disoriented in the powder until I could free a ski or a pole and recuperate for a minute before heaving myself up to tumble some more, then plodding back up on my shaky legs. At the end of the day, I should admit, those pretty parallel S marks also included my own long erratic body-skid tracks. Not that it bothered me much. I sat with the others again that night shivering in all my clothes in the dregs of pink alpine glow until the moon rose. I was happy to be there, and happier yet that the next day we'd be heading back.

When, in the morning, I shouldered my pack for the long journey home I found I could not lean forward to manage the heavy load the way I'd done for all those uphill miles. When I stood still my skis slipped backwards from under me without warning, and when I started to move they yanked me forward like Dino Flintstone on a leash. I fell, wrestled to the surface, and fell again. The others glided down ahead of me off the saddle, out of the basin, and into the woods where, beneath the trees crowding the trail, deep icy craters had formed over the course of the winter as snow accumulated on the tree limbs. The tree wells had been there on the way up, but they hadn't posed a problem. With downhill acceleration they posed a problem—for me. I watched the others ski into and out of them, side-slipping around the flayed top like skiing the edge of a cereal bowl or performing a trick in a skateboard park. Whoopty do! I didn't know how to sideslip. I followed their tracks and fell some more. Each time I fell, I rolled onto my belly, face in snow, to have enough leverage to stand with the heavy pack. I steeled myself, every muscle full-throttle taut to rise slowly, steadily, onto my feet without falling again. Then I paused to catch my breath. My legs ached and threatened to cramp, but I'd taken four aspirin and already planned to ignore the pain. I'd ski for a minute or two, then fall again. Up and then down. Up and then down. Over and over and over. I began to count: fifteen, twenty, twenty-five, thirty falls. My legs left off aching and tremored instead, like a sewing machine needle left running, thread knotting. The others waited for me at first, and they recommended that I glue the climbing skins back onto the bottom of the skis for friction. So I did. After that, I fell just as often, but I fell more slowly.

By lunch time, I had fallen more than fifty times and, wisely, I had stopped counting. I was happy for the break and happier yet that someone had some squares of chocolate left to share. My hands shook so hard that I could barely eat, even though I didn't feel the least bit cold. The others joked and shoveled fistfuls of cracker crumbs into their mouths, and bounced on their skis, anxious to go. They packed their empty baggies and cinched their laces, and I thought of saying something. I need to sit down, maybe. I need a hot drink. Something. I was working up to saying it as I pawed the wrapper of one last chocolate. But before I could, they were off and moving again. And I was alone.

I rounded a bend and emerged back onto the sidehill for the long slip home. I'd made my peace with the skins, and I maintained an in-between speed at which I could, largely, keep my balance. Only the tree wells remained challenging, in part because on the sidehill more snow accumulated on the downhill side of the tree than the uphill, so the wells were growing deeper. I concentrated on my feet, followed in the tracks of the others, slowly into the well and back out. Not falling. Concentrating. I watched my feet in the double track for so long that a progression of train song snippets began to play in my head. *She'll be comin' round the mountain when she comes. She'll be comin' round the mountain when she* ... I fell mid-lyric. I heard my knee snap, loud and incongruous against the soft rippling of the creek below, as I went over sideways into the tree well, and I hung upside down, suspended, ski tips on one side, tails on the other.

These days, despite my reconstructed knee, I run most winter days in the chain-tracks of the road grader after it plows or on the slick driven-over patches of ice. I pull off my hood to escape the deafening patter of too-wet snow on Gore-tex and keep on running down the valley until I emerge from a forested tunnel directly across from where Devore Creek pours out of its narrow gorge into Lake Chelan. I wouldn't be able to see Ten Mile Pass from here if I tried. But I know it's there. It would be easier to discard the shimmering memory, to replace it with, say, the arthroscopic photo of my shredded ligament, if it weren't for the fact that it's not just my story, or just mine and Laurie's; it's all knotted up with our friends and neighbors and the place we call home. Bob told me, shortly after my accident, that he'd once hurt his knee and that I'd get through it. And he was right. Today I ran for an hour and passed only three people: Jonathan working at his portable saw mill, Bob riding his bike to check electric meters, and Tom delivering propane house to house. We share the complicated memory like we once shared the whole brilliant sun-sinking universe and a cold six-pack of beer, like we share the tiny steep-walled valley, sometimes unbearably lonely, sometimes unspeakably lovely. Maybe it's the smallness or the loneliness or the beauty, or maybe it's just the years spent together that have nurtured in me loyalty every bit as fierce and stubborn as my independence once was. Still, every time I run to the lake, I look over my shoulder toward Devore Creek in disbelief and wonder: what was I thinking?

I know exactly what I was thinking after I fell. I was thinking how beautiful the sky was, blue like the clearest water, deep and inviting and restful. So very restful. I dangled in silence for a long time thinking I might take a little nap, while Jack London wended his way back toward me, marching off the pages of my grade school reading textbook. This, Jack London reminded me, is how people die. Then, at last, I screamed.

I unclipped the hip belt of my pack, still hanging upside down, and fought my arms from the shoulder straps. I rocked myself back and forth using my stomach muscles to hold myself in position long enough to free my boots from the ski bindings. I landed in a heap and tried to stand. And then I knew. My right knee shifted in place, a gruesome double-jointed stunt. I grabbed aspirin and water and my ski poles. I left my pack and the borrowed skis leaning against the tree. And I began to walk. If my knee did not hurt exactly, it didn't work exactly either. I hobbled through the deep snow, post-holing or body-plowing, sitting on my butt and sliding. And I continued to yell. I had no idea how far ahead the rest of them might be, but I knew how the sound of the creek traveled, and I had some faith that my voice might travel as well. I yelled, and I began to recognize my own folly. Yelling for help into a wide empty expanse was easier, by far, than asking for help up close had been. But I knew it was either too late or too early for regrets. It was time to get moving.

After an hour or two, I decided I'd have to pace my voice, so I yelled only every few minutes. At first I was democratic about it, hollering one name, then the next: *Bob, Jonathan, Tom, Laurie.* Then just: *Help.* After a while I gave in and just repeated: *Laurie Laurie Laurie Laurie.*

The sun disappeared behind thick watery gray clouds, nothing like the familiar bluish inversion clouds, thin as tracing paper, but dense and dead serious. No chance now of staying the night. If it were to snow several feet, I'd probably die. For one thing, Laurie and I had divided the gear, so I had the fuel and she had the stove, which meant I had no way to melt snow for drinking water. More to the point, Laurie had the tent, and I had no idea how to build a snow shelter. I had to make it down, plain and simple, and while mostly it was going well—sometimes I slid on my rain pants, sometimes I post-holed through the snow, only sinking a bit, but enough to yank my unfastened knee this way and that—my biggest fear was the ice balls. I didn't think the crooked leg could hold me steady enough to cross all those chutes.

Finally, from the top of a small treeless knob, I could see down through the trees to where Laurie loitered, her skis still facing down the trail. Even from a distance she looked uncertain and a little embarrassed. After all, waiting for someone was against the unspoken code.

"Hey!" I cried.

"Hey!" she hollered back, and she stepped forward on one ski. Now that she'd seen me, she could head on down the hill.

"I hurt my knee," I screamed.

She continued to nod happily.

"I hurt my knee," I screamed again. This time she heard, the screechy tone at least. Or maybe she noticed, at last, that I no longer had skis or a pack.

She waited for me to catch up. "I should go get the others," she said.

I must have looked terrified. I'd already been left behind once. I didn't think I could face it again. "You'll never catch them," I said.

Laurie nodded, and I saw that the situation was serious, at least as serious as I'd imagined. From here on out, another five miles, I followed Laurie's footsteps in earnest. She took off her skis and strapped them to her pack, then kicked solid steps into the deep snow as new snow began to fall. I stepped with my left leg and lifted the dangly-knee right leg with my hand to set it in the tracks and so we continued for several hours. I know this the way you know old family stories—because I've been told—not because I remember those hours. Once I caught up with Laurie I took no more responsibility for my own well-being, but drifted in and out of reality. I blacked out several times.

"Are you OK?" she asked.

I nodded and grimaced.

"You should sit and rest," she said. "Let me splint it. Or at least wrap it."

I shook my head, afraid that if I did, my knee would swell and lose what little mobility it had.

"OK," she said, and stomped ahead, turning occasionally to watch me trudge behind.

Then came the ice ball chutes. It was hard to see them coming through the heavy snow now falling, but then there they were.

"Stay here," Laurie said, placing one hand on my shoulder for emphasis, then she balanced across, set down her pack, and doubled back to walk me across. I took her hand and we forged on. One down. Many more to go.

So there it is: the lesson I learned when I was twenty-three wasn't that actions have consequences, but that trust is, well, trustworthy.

The sky darkened, not just with clouds, but eventually with nightfall. By that time we were on flat ground, one headlamp between us, breaking through several inches of new snow.

Laurie stopped.

We'd come to the sloughs, the swampy braided river channels we had crossed on Day One. Back then we had balanced so easily on the brittle limbs. In the dark, now almost total, and with my knee joint going every-which-way, crossing on those limbs was out of the question. Calling for help to get Bob to row back across the river to fetch us would work once we crossed these sloughs but not before.

"We have to wade," I said.

The murky water was topped with slushy ice and still-yellow cottonwood leaves and downed logs suspended in a jackstraw. I did not think much before leaping. What choice did I have? I was weary of the darkness, the pain, even tired of Laurie's concern, weary mostly of my own stupid rugged individualism. Even Jack London ditched the pose young, I reminded myself. He grew up and turned socialist and championed the dispossessed.

I leapt into the waist-deep water, warmer than the air, and half-waded, half-swam across before I looked back to see Laurie hesitating on the shore.

"Come on," I yelled and waded partway back to hold her wrist and pull her through the dark water. One slough. Two sloughs. We clambered out and stood by the edge of the river, hollering for Bob to show up to row us back across in the darkness of a starless sky.

And he did.

Ten years later, Bob and I worked together building our house, Laurie's and mine. We were nailing rafters into place, using the tight-grained local fir Jonathan had milled from the trees on our property, lumber that shunned nails with stubborn vengeance. We'd given up on pre-drilling, so now I was concentrating on beating twenty penny nails in hard.

"You know that time you hurt your knee," Bob said.

I stopped work and held still, hammer in hand.

"Uh huh," I said.

During surgery I remembered, a group of surgeons had hammered long and hard to fit the parts of my reconstructed ligament in place. Now the hardware had held for so long I'd forgotten it was there.

"Well, I never hurt my knee like *that*," he said.

I went back to work for a while without a word, knowing those nails, too, would hold snug, and that within a few years the house—like loyalty and forgiveness and tender new love— would seem so sturdy as to have grown up on its own.

"Yeah, well," I said at last. "It's a hundred percent now. I mean, it worked out fine."

What's Heaven without a Gate?

Approaching Crystal Cove, you knew something was afoot. The place was an anomaly, an undeveloped swath of land wedged between the cliché California beaches: wall-to-wall beach blankets, roller skaters on the promenade, radios blaring, video arcades and ice cream shops, high-dollar rentals. Here, unexpectedly, right on Highway 1 was a sweep of open hillside, yellow grass waving in the wind. My dad took a hard right on an unmarked road, steep and twisty, tightly lined with eucalyptus trees, and in a matter of seconds, we were there: a place entirely apart.

A handful of small cabins lined the bluff and huddled close on the beach behind makeshift sea walls for when, during the highest tides, breakers crashed at the doorstep. They were shanties of various sorts, unfinished and artsy, flat roofed and cedar sided and painted bright seaside blues and whites and greens, adorned with various beach treasures: nets and buoys, shells and glass, driftwood and palm fronds. The cabins, built in the 1930s, were authentic representations of "vernacular beach architecture" or so historians decided when, in the late 1970s, locals lobbied to have them listed on the National Historic Registry in an ingenious but ultimately unsuccessful attempt to save themselves from eviction. The cabins had no fences, and if the locals were not always friendly, they were watchful. It was the kind of place, my mom marvels still, where if my brother and sister and I left our beach buckets below the high tide line, someone would surely return them to the cabin before they washed away.

79

Crystal Cove had been part of the Irvine Ranch, one of the largest privately owned tracts of land in California. J. I. Irvine Jr., who had inherited the land from his father, a gold rusher, had tolerated squatters at the cove since the 1920s. He stipulated only that, upon his death, the land should go to the state for preservation. When he died in 1947, his legacy was left to a corporation, the Irvine Company, that had other priorities— donating land for a University of California campus, for example—and Crystal Cove was more or less ignored for three decades. Because the situation was legally tenuous, the cabins remained unimproved through the postwar boom and beyond. I'd known since I was a very small child that they'd someday be gone. In my mind this loomed with the same certainty as high school and marriage and USC in the Rose Bowl and eventually nuclear annihilation. Crystal Cove would go to the state.

We lived sixty long miles inland, but my parents scrimped mightily so we could go to Crystal Cove each year for a week or two, during which I fantasized about living there full-time. The Crystal Cove locals lived the good life, it seemed. We watched them curiously, surreptitiously, and with abject jealousy. They launched catamarans at sunset, clean beautiful people laughing and drinking. "Crystal Cove Yacht Club—Members Only" read a hand-painted tongue-in-cheek sign in front of a small rickety driftwood shelter sporting a hand-painted "restroom" sign pointing toward the ocean. Just behind the yacht club sat an outbuilding on which hung the most famous landmark on the beach, a rusty clock, hands permanently rusted in place, below which a small sign read: "Crystal Cove Standard Time—Set your clocks back to 1930."

Stehekin, I realized after settling in, is a lot like Crystal Cove. Visitors arrive daily. They marvel at the beauty of the valley, the conifer smells, the calendar views, the timeless small-town simplicity. It is common enough in tourist towns for locals to begrudge the visitors, even as they eke a living from them, but this is not West Yellowstone, not Maui. Locals allow the visitors space to fish and swim and camp and wobble on rented bicycles in front of our pickups because it's what the place demands of us. If I leave a dish at a potluck, like my childhood buckets on the beach, it will show up at the post office for me to retrieve the next day. Tourists, I imagine, must sometimes wonder about how nice it must be to live in such a seemingly unsullied place.

Seemingly. For decades Stehekin has been mired in controversy. The idea was, I suppose, inevitable: such a pristine place should be preserved for future generations. So thirty years ago the National Park Service took over jurisdiction of most of the area from the U.S. Forest Service, a move that protected tens of thousands of acres from logging and prevented a highway from being constructed along the current route of the Pacific Crest Trail. But it was not an entirely welcome change. While the charter legislation protected the right to private property, Park Service land acquisition—more preservation—was given priority. Between 1968 and 1973, 2.4 million federal dollars were spent to acquire 986 acres, leaving just 650 acres in Stehekin in private hands. (Today the number is closer to 425.) How, exactly, this happened is debatable. Willing sellers? Threats of eminent domain? It's the stuff of long-held grudges, lawsuits, and fierce opinions. Whatever the truth, the fact that some Stehekenites remain distrustful of the government, ever mindful of the possibility of eviction, makes perfectly good sense. Two million acres of federally designated wilderness surround us now. The conservationists effectively won.

And, of course, it's a damned good thing they did. Who hasn't seen how private land goes to hell in a handbasket? In California, as most places, laissez-faire reads strip mall. Nearly every inch. What is there to see there? Stores. What is there to do there? Shop. The government might squander money, and make misguided decisions, but it doesn't put in the Gap and Old Navy and Trader Joe's. That, in part, is what happened to Crystal Cove. The beach itself went to the state in 1979—1,898 acres for $32.6 million— but the outlying areas, those undeveloped yellow hillsides, the last stronghold for indigenous species, went to the highest bidder. Strip malls, condos, golf courses, they're all there. The stuff of a bad TV melodrama. So predictably grotesque.

And it could have been worse. A few years back, Republican Governor Pete Wilson proposed a high-end "eco-resort" right on the beach, where concessionaires could charge $375-$700 per person per night for upscale tourists to stay in the renovated cabins and enjoy amenities like valet parking, a fitness center, a restaurant, and three swimming pools. Wilson's excuse was the prohibitive cost of restoration. Granted, the Crystal Cove shanties, protected by their official historic designation, did pose a problem that way. None of them had any insulation. I doubt many had heat. Mold and rot welcome here! More worrisome, perhaps, were the outmoded or nonexistent septic systems. Vernacular does come with complications. The upside of Wilson's outrageous proposal was to galvanize his opponents, conservationists and locals alike, so that now there is talk of non-profit tide pool interpretive programs, an artist-in-residency-program, a dolphin research outpost. All high-minded and, I think, exemplary ideas. Meanwhile, the cabin owners received their final eviction notices, and in 2001, after one last sunset swim party, moved out. You've probably caught on by now. I'm mourning for Crystal Cove. I can't help it. Even if the very best options come to pass, I still think something will have been lost. When we were kids, a tall sinewy unsmiling man rode a one-speed bike along the potholed pavement to the beach every morning, a poodle between the handlebars. He walked with the poodle for some distance in the fog until, eventually, he stopped to toss bread crumbs into a cloud of feverish gulls. He was silent and menacing, and scared us kids a lot. We never spoke to him, but we expected him like we expected the spouting dolphins passing beyond the waves, the nasturtiums lining the ramshackle wooden boardwalk, the catamarans at sunset. And we thought of him as our own. Whether he thought of us as his own, I can't say. But we liked to think he did.

At the base of the hill, as you approached Crystal Cove, was a large pipe-welded gate, and over the years, there were various plans for getting through it: hidden keys and forgotten codes. (A gate? A gate? Appalling, I know, but then paradise is always defined by exclusivity. What's heaven without a gate?) Just beyond the gate were a long row of dilapidated garages, in which lived the poodle man, the unofficial St. Peter for the cove. He had no cabin, no garden. He had only this self-appointed job and for that he was tolerated, even embraced. As a kid, I liked to believe that if the key or code didn't work, the poodle man would let us in. He wouldn't smile, but he would swing the gate wide to let our station wagon through. He was part of the fold, and we were too. Live and let live. With an unspoken helping of kindness. That was the real code at Crystal Cove.

I know the hard truth. Things fall apart. You can't step in the river twice. Nostalgia is fervent and revisionist, naïve, and probably unhealthy, and my longing for Crystal Cove before the state took over or for Stehekin before the park was created is a little like well-heeled Miami exiles longing for Cuba before Castro: a mythic place that no longer exists, one you might not even choose to return to if you could. Whether the result of earnest intention or grievous wrongdoing or the everyday rotations of earth around sun, things change. Still, Crystal Cove haunts me.

Part of the problem is that I see Crystal Cove as a harbinger of sorts, an omen. Crystal Cove is precisely what I *don't* want for Stehekin: eviction notices forcibly served. But it is equally true that Stehekin is precisely what I *don't* want for Crystal Cove, the touristification of everything. I worry that what Stehekin loses, by small measures, in the protective hands of government is its own unique character.

Here's what I'm thinking: let private ownership run amok, and—duh!—a place gets ruined. But let public ownership run amok, and a place gets ruined, too. Land preserved can become like a memorial or a mausoleum, a place to be solemnly observed and respected. Hands off! It's stuffy and static and completely unrealistic because we are changing the land, always, even while we stand aside and watch; we've already changed it, and we're part of the equation, and it's no time to step back. There are plenty of familiar examples: new super-catastrophic fires, if left to burn, sterilize soil and prevent regeneration; noxious weed proliferation endangers native plants; wildlife populations spiral out of control where predators have been eliminated. We have an obligation to step in, at least some of the time. And more to the point—what I'm trying to get at here—is the fact that even as we change the land, the land is changing us. Most of us belong to certain little places, not the other way around, and to loose our hold, to give in to bigness of any political persuasion is to feel untethered, adrift. Found, and mostly, lost.

There were tide pools at Crystal Cove, several sets of them; the first rocks, we called them, and the second rocks, and the third, and so on. There, in the years before his early untimely death, my dad could cast his line into the surf, and my mom could collect seashells to save in peanut butter jars back home in the garage, shelves and shelves of them. More than three decades have passed. The rocks are still there. Ditto the anemones and the dolphins. This is not, for once, an elegy for nature lost. The marine life at Crystal Cove, save the abalone, has proved remarkably resilient. In this story, a twist on the defining story of our time, nature is still there, but the magic, at least as we knew it, is gone.

Some people I know, some I admire very much, like to espouse the Native American ideal that no land should be owned. Let nature run the show, they say. Meanwhile, developers with fewer scruples make cell phone real estate transactions on the chair lifts, collect their profits, and pour the pavement. Let the free market run the show, they say. There ought to be some middle ground, I think, a way for a handful of people to hole up in a tiny undeveloped cranny and make it their own, to develop a little maybe, but not a lot. Maybe it's too much to ask anymore. Maybe we've outgrown this never-ending game of last-best-place. We've played too many times. There are too few hiding places left.

Ah, but there are some. There still are too-dry deserts and too-wet beaches and too-brushy hollows where if there's a will there's a way. People carve out little niches all the time, and I am always awed by them: by their determination, their willingness to make do. I want to say to them: stay hidden, stay as long as you possibly can. But fair warning, when you are found—when *we* are found, and we will be—come forward gracefully. A place apart it no longer is. It never really was.

After my dad died, the family did not go to Crystal Cove for a handful of years, a blip in time for my younger brother and sister but a meaningful stretch for me—the difference between sweet innocence and scowling adolescence. By the time we returned I noted the noise of the highway, an omnipresent roar, and the polluted water running down the canyon from the storm drains on the highway and into the ocean. The place felt suddenly false to me, tucked as it was into the seething maw of Californian humanity. False it was. It was not separate from the world, of course, but held afloat on a web of entanglements that spanned from the gold rush to the governor's mansion.

The half-moon cove that had stretched forever when I was a kid, the third rocks such a distance, turned out to be no longer than a couple miles, a frustratingly short distance for an aspiring cross-country runner. On my sixteenth birthday, I ran in the morning early, passing the poodle man and no one else, on the hard sand below the high-tide mark. Then back in front of the cabin I peeled off my shoes and socks and waded into the surf to swim. From out past the waves, I could look back at the spattering of shacks on the shore like the blue orb of earth from space: so small, insignificant really, part of the larger solar system, and the galaxy, and the universe. There's some comfort, I suppose, in knowing that we're just a tiny part of something bigger. At least it is fashionable, in a bumper sticker way, to believe that there is. But there is sadness, too, though we rarely let our adult selves feel it, in knowing that there is always another wave coming, a bigger wave that will surely overtake us, and the only thing to do is to hold your ground, bracing yourself in the churn, watching the horizon, waiting. By the time I turned sixteen, I knew the rules of the game. I wallowed in the fleeting visceral pleasure: warm sweat meets cold surf. I stayed in the water as long as I possibly could, until I heard my mother calling me from the porch, then I caught a ride from the crest of a wave right onto the sand and ran to pack my bags and drive away, newly licensed, past the gate, and back into the wide world, racing for home.

Postscript:
Starting in 2006, the Crystal Cove cottages now "authentically restored" to the 1935-1955 era became available for the public to rent for reasonable rates (as little as $33 per person per night), through the California Cove Alliance, a non-profit partner with California State Parks. Reservations open at 8:00 a.m. sharp on the first of the month for the seventh month in advance (i.e.,

on January 1 for the entire month of July). Try to rent any room in any cabin in any month, summer and winter, and they are booked, usually, by 8:03 a.m. (What's heaven without a gate?) A friend recently secured a room in a dorm-style cabin by applying for a cancellation last minute. She watched the sunset from the cabin deck, and reported that the magic, for those who get lucky, is still there.

Lost and Found

Ɑ

On my first day of college, my roommate kicked me out before meeting me. I was a thousand miles from home and mired in an ill-fated love affair with an older man, which I had recently—and temporarily, as it turned out—called to a halt. I was shy and serious and wowed, despite everything, by western Oregon: the greenery, the river running right through town. Right through town! I dropped off my things and walked away from the dorms and out along the Willamette, awestruck, for miles. By the time I returned, near dusk, I'd been kicked out.

"She's in my sorority," my would-be-roommate explained with a shrug about my replacement. "You can move across the hall."

Why couldn't she move across the hall? I ought to have argued. After all, one room looked out on green Frisbee-game lawns, the other on the narrow asphalt loading dock of the cafeteria.

"OK," I said. Loading dock it was.

That rejection, it turned out, like so many, was a stroke of extraordinary luck. Sherry, my new roommate, was as shy and serious as me. We both came from elsewhere: she from the sprawly suburbs of Chicago and I from the suburbs of L.A.—Lost Angeles, I liked to call it—sprawlier yet, and probably because of where we'd come from, we both nurtured a fanatic obsession with the outdoors. If we didn't talk a lot about where we came from, we didn't really need to. We talked about where we were, and where we might be going, not in the career sense, but in a real sense: the rivers, the mountains, the deserts. Sherry might be shy and serious, but whenever we ventured outside, anywhere, even along the paved bike paths and manicured park lawns by the Willamette, her long stride grew longer, her blue eyes bluer, her smile suddenly wide, maniacal even. She went barefoot long into the fall and hitchhiked to Rainbow Gatherings deep in the forest, where once she caught poison oak from a campfire, a dangerously serious case. She always returned to tell the tale. And she always grinned when she did. And once, when the older man was briefly back in the picture, he and Sherry and I drove to the ocean. It was winter and raining and the first time she had seen the Pacific. We were, all of us, elated.

❧

On a winter day twenty years later, Laurie and I drive north on Highway 395 toward Bend from Gardnerville, Nevada. Snowflakes the size of silver-dollar crepes flutter toward us as we drive, alone on the road, climbing the piney flats, dropping to sage, chasing the smell of juniper like the holy grail. A *quik stop* for coffee. A credit card swipe for gas. The sun sets as the moon rises and the snow slows to expose a blue hem of sky bleeding pink among the pines. My friend in Gardnerville keeps saying she wants to move to Bend, and as we drive north, anticipation mounting, it seems like a stroke of genius. Bend? Of course!

By the time we reach the glowing outskirts of town, we are travel addled and lost. Which off-ramp do we take? So much has changed since we last came through, five years ago. We exit the highway and enter a new upscale shopping development. The purposely winding ways spin us in circles—where could we possibly be?—while the too-familiar monster storefronts signal that we could be anywhere: Seattle or Chicago, Lost Angeles even. I know. I know. It's the story of our time, our generation—not gentrification so much as generic nation—a dead-horse theme so tiresome I promise not to beat it except to say that, in the moment, it makes us want to get the hell out. I make a mental note to tell my friend in Gardnerville: forget it. Bend, like so many places, has been found. And, therefore, lost.

Q

The things Sherry and I did not discuss in our dorm room were precisely the same things, I suspect, that our former roommates did discuss: clothes, makeup, parties, malls, movies. Even boys. Though, in hindsight, it would have done both Sherry and me some good to talk about men. I was devastated at the end of the older-man saga. I wanted to buy a TV and wallow for a while. Sherry said, simply: No. Instead she signed me up to volunteer with a disabled child.

"I'm not interested," I told her.

"I already signed you up," she told me.

"OK," I said.

And I headed for the river, where so many trees, so much water, had felt, since my arrival in Oregon, like redemption, like landing in a second-chance universe, a softer, sweeter one. As a kid, I'd watched smog layers settle on the L.A. horizon like salad dressing ingredients—gray atop brown atop burnt orange—and mountain ridges disappear with pages on the calendar. The most distant range vanished in May, the next closest in June. By July even the knobby hills in town sunk in the soup. In August, the summer before college, I'd commuted on a freeway so thick with traffic and pollution I couldn't see the bumper in front of me. There's no way to overstate this: arriving in Oregon, for me, had been like Dorothy entering the Technicolor Land of Oz.

So you can imagine my shock when, in the wake of my first heartbreak, the green grew suddenly suffocating. Like Dorothy, I began to miss my home. It was a shameful, hard-to-admit kind of missing complicated by the dreadful state of nature that I had left in my home state. It wasn't hard to admit that I missed my family and friends back home, not at all, but the fact that I was beginning to ache for Southern California was disgraceful, I thought. Like failure.

Around the same time, Sherry met a local mill worker, handsome and fit and vegetarian, and fell hard in love. She got pregnant. Then married. I'd stand up as her maid of honor, watch her son as he grew, watch the second one come along, and watch the divorce before I'd graduate and move away. In the last weeks before her wedding, Sherry and I drove up the Mackenzie and over the pass. We rented cross-country skis, an extravagant splurge, and slogged merrily up unmarked trails, over downed logs, across narrow gurgling creeks. Here it was, yet another magical world. How many might lurk yet, I marveled, on this seemingly lost-cause planet?

I skied among orange-barked ponderosas, with sun on the snow and—this! this!—sun on my skin. Despite the fact that I'd already pledged allegiance to the rainy west side, despite the fact that I had many years of drippiness ahead of me, I felt a delicious sun-baked affinity for the desert in winter. I already knew the problem with admitting to my California roots. I'd faced the knee-jerk Oregonian reaction dozens of times. But I couldn't help it. The east side of the mountains felt like home.

Turns out, during those same years Laurie lived a ski bum life at Mt. Bachelor, baking cinnamon rolls by night and learning to telemark by day. Me, I was ditching Eugene for Bend on a regular basis with a pair of garage-sale cross-country skis and a sack lunch. After Laurie and I hooked up, we moved semi-annually as seasonal laborers, planting trees, clearing trails, clinging to a life spent almost entirely outdoors, and trying, maybe, to earn with our sweat what we had not earned by birth: a sense of belonging. Since Laurie grew up in drippy Seattle and I grew up on the edge of the Mojave, we vacillated for several years between wet and dry—summer in the North Cascades, winter in Flagstaff, high, dry and junipery, an approximation of Bend—until we finally settled down. But the romance of the high desert remained, for both of us. Laurie kept a stock supply of juniper berries in the ash tray of her sun-roofed Tercel, so the smell seeped in through the vents each time the heater ran, and she collected bottles of Bombay Sapphire, the gin with a juniper twig etched in the blue glass. When it came time to build our cabin we decided to import knotty juniper logs. As much as anything, juniper was a symbol of what we used to be, what we could have been. Of possibility.

Of course, I know that junipers are not all symbol and gin spice. They're opportunists, swiping precious water from native grasses and shrubs, ruining ranchland. No longer at the mercy of wildfire, they encroach and overpopulate. Even where they have been selectively removed, chained away, they raise their berry-drooping limbs again, stubborn and triumphant. I ought to scorn them, I know, ought to file them under "undesirable," with knapweed and toadflax and dumpster-fed raccoons. But I can't. It's not because I don't know all this about junipers that I feel an affinity for them. It's because I do know.

The cold hard truth is that I don't belong either. Save the Native Americans, none of us do. If I allow myself to think this way too long, all hope is lost. Instead I try to grab a foothold. When the air smells like juniper, no matter how my inner naturalist protests, I rejoice. Like the notes of an old song that unearth a sweet lost memory, the smell makes my knees go weak. That's gotta count for something.

❧

In the years after college, Sherry and I kept in touch, off and on, through eraser-smudged phone numbers and letters scratched on the back of recycled junk mail until eventually, inevitably, she dropped out of sight. Such it was with friendship for me in those years. My own address changed more than twenty times in the course of a decade. When people got lost, I figured, they were gone for good. I was wrong.

It's on our winter trip to Bend that we run into Sherry, out of the blue, at a book reading. She's changed her last name, an easy way to fall out of touch, and I've published a book, an easy name-in-the-paper way to fall back in, so it is without effort or intrigue that we've found each other again. We stop for a beer at a sports bar far from the shiny gentrified center of town and settle back into friendship like a comfy old couch, an unspoken affinity, not knowing what the other is thinking—it was never quite that way with Sherry—but knowing at least, always, what matters most: rivers, mountains, deserts. We make a plan to cross-country ski together in the morning before my afternoon reading then return to her house to crash on the floor.

"I have lots of room," she says. And I am grateful. Even a $35 motel room stretches our meager laborers' budget.

The ski is great: three hours of new snow skittering, sun-breaks and solace, logs to navigate on the downhill stretches and icy spots on the up. We finish in the nick of time. Laurie and I head out to the afternoon reading and return, exhausted, in time to share supper with Sherry and her older son. She has made vegetarian soup and lit candles, and it is a fine and quiet evening, a chance to get to know the high school senior I last knew as a toddler, an avid skier now, considering colleges in Montana and Colorado, using precisely the same criterion his mother and I once used: where are there mountains?

At 8:30, as I prepare to clear dishes and collapse in my sleeping bag, Sherry stands and stretches.

"Well, shall we go?" she asks.

"Go where?" I say, though I have an inkling. While we were skiing she had talked about a hike she'd like to do with us, but I had, I thought, begged off. We have to drive seven hours tomorrow, I'd said. I'm not interested, I may as well have said. But as I look at her in the flickering candlelight, I recognize the look in her eyes. I already signed you up, she may as well have said.

"Smith Rocks," she says.

I nearly groan. Generic Smith Rocks. As if we've never been there.

"OK," I say.

We drive for an hour, then walk for two more, headlamps pocketed under just-enough moon, in city shoes, tennies, skidding on ball-bearing gravel, wheezing in the unfamiliar altitude, gazing agog at the horizon swept wide, stars twinkling, the canyons silhouetted, their black edges sure and clean as pen strokes, and the river below molding the landscape as if with a putty knife. My mood has lifted, and suddenly, I can think of no better place to be. Sherry leads the way, climbing switchbacks in long easy strides. At a junction, she pauses to sip water.

"Monkey Face," she says, gesturing to the famous high point on the ridge. "Do you want to go all the way?"

"Yes!" Laurie exclaims. She is giddy now, I think, with exhaustion and re-piqued infatuation with this place.

"Sure," I say.

Sherry's face breaks into that familiar maniacal grin. When she starts back up, her pace redoubles.

In nearly twenty years as a single mom, Sherry has learned to eke out these small-scale adventures. Her teaching job leaves her precious little free time, so on weekdays she hits the stairstepper. When she's there, I wonder if the locals on the sweat-sheened machines look at her askance. Though Sherry's no Californian, she does look the part: tan, blond, muscled. She's an outsider, they might reasonably think, an encroacher. They'd know nothing of what she's sacrificed to be where she is, or how the landscape's loneliness and exaltedness mirror her spirit. They wouldn't understand how she's better for where she is, and the place is better because of immigrants like her—like so many of us—who love it with weak-kneed passion.

We continue to climb, and from near the top, we can see the whole flat plateau, moonlight exposed, and the few headlights at that time of night, at that time of year, bold and purposeful, destined for somewhere. In the distance, city lights huddle against the dark, no match for the broad largely empty expanse of desert. I revise my mental note to my friend in Gardnerville. It's not so bad, I decide to say. It hasn't changed that much. At least not yet.

Still climbing. The three of us silent now. But for the wind and the scuffing of shoes on rock, the whole wide universe is silent.

Some changes are more dire than others. Pavement is forever, say the bumper stickers back home. And god knows we can do with less of it. Pregnant at nineteen, that's forever too. It's not, I think, that changes don't matter. It's just that I can't help but admire when survivors—like juniper, like Sherry—take root and flourish despite the changes, sometimes because of the changes. I can't help but marvel at the unexpected delights that lurk in the crannies of our planet and, often enough, in the wrongness of my own smog-damaged ideas.

A place that is found—known, discovered, even developed— is not always lost.

A person who is lost is not lost forever.

Not as long as that inexplicable connection draws us back across time and distance, out of a warm house and onto the scaly steep trails of a sub-freezing night to a place both hard-earned and gifted to us, amongst rocks and stars that predate our arrival by eons and will outlast us by at least as long. We climb the last shortened switchback and stand beside Monkey Face.

It's not the first time we have seen it—not by a long shot—but it makes no difference. We are, all of us, elated.

Nature Is Our Cotton Ball Bunny

The artist stands in front of thirty-five of us who have come to the lakeshore on this hot summer evening for an opening at the community art gallery. My mom sits at a picnic table with a couple of her friends, all of them here on vacation. Kids are playing tag. Adults are seated at the picnic tables or cross-legged on the lawn listening politely to the artist's speech, which they hope, like a sermon, will be blessedly short and fleetingly inspiring. In that order.

The artist speaks of the importance of historical influences and of stretching the bounds of those influences, which by the look of his work, he's done plenty. He speaks of "essences." He uses the word "ineffable." He is, in general, long on whys and short on hows. I am interested, genuinely, in his talk, but I get distracted when a three-year-old approaches offering me a fistful of garden-plucked flowers and wanting to climb in my lap. I don't hear everything he says, but I'm pretty sure I hear him say this:

"There's a lot of art in craft, and a lot of craft in art."

The artist is amiable, and he offers this innocuous phrase with a shrug as if to say: no offense intended. I glance over at Jean. She is scowling. Just as I thought: whether or not the artist intended offense, he offered it. I'm pretty sure what Jean heard is this: craft is what we've got in Stehekin. Art is something more.

For Jean, it's the kind of presumption that rankles. Jean studied art in college back in the sixties before she migrated west, then farther into the woods until she landed here on the far reaches of civilization with her husband-to-be twenty-five years ago. Over time, she has mastered the required skills: wood splitting, snow shoveling, gardening, canning, cooking. She is a strict vegetarian and a staunch environmentalist who has been president of the local school board and has worked seasonally for the National Park Service.

Though Jean has several avocations, art—specifically fabric art—remains her vocation. She sews quilts and wall hangings, uniquely imagined and impeccably stitched, making use of a myriad of fabrics, often scraps sent by an acquaintance who owns an upholstery shop in Greenwich Village. In some ways, for Jean, fabric art is the perfect combination of inclination and philosophy. Traditionally the work of poor women, fabric art is both feminist and utilitarian. Taken at its best, it is a renaissance of sorts, a profound act of respect, an art form that is growing in reputation. (Even as we gather in Stehekin, an exhibit of quilts by women from small-town Alabama—"The Quilts of Gee's Bend"—is on display at the Whitney.) Still Jean's medium is often dismissed, tossed into the craft bin along with whittling and glass blowing. Jean is plain sick of it, I think. Her ire, like her passion, runs deep.

Tonight's speaker, a painter and print maker well known in places like New York and San Francisco, is a friend of Jean's, and they have had this art-versus-craft debate before. Jean started this community art gallery, she remains on the committee, and she's the one who invited him to speak.

The day has been hot, and this reprieve at the lake is welcome. Bugs hover over the water and an occasional fish surfaces. The punky smell of distant forest fires lingers. Before tonight's talk, the largish crowd milled around inside, waiting their turn to file through the tiny room where monthly shows are hung.

This show, like most, is a mishmash of local talent: woodwork, photography, pen and ink, some of it the fruit of years of commitment and some of it the self-expression of dabblers. The gallery reflects the democratic nature of life in this very small town. The same spirit informs the weekly baseball games where eight-year-olds take swings alongside teenagers and a handful of codgers. Sure, the teenagers' faces betray a tiny measure of impatience while lobs are pitched and the ball peters into play and the little kid runs it out charging fist-clenched toward the grassless depression at first base. But they don't complain. They can't be choosy if they want to field full teams. Besides, which of the teenagers didn't start out that way? And did they want a game or not?

So it is with the gallery. Of course we must tread more gingerly here because we are adults now, thin-skinned, with tender feelings at stake. Good manners are the order of the day. Folks enter the gallery, murmur their approval, and queue up for the lemonade thermos and the paper plate of cookies.

Most of tonight's guests discern the difference between the work of the veterans like Jean and that of the neophytes. But not all of them. Occasionally the colored-pencil rendition of the forest captures something of the yellow light in autumn that a visitor recalls with wistfulness, a visitor who perhaps can no longer stay this far north into the cold season. Or the mountain in the photograph outshines whatever artistic intention does or does not accompany it. Would you look at that? we say. We admire the mountain for what it is, and we are grateful to the photographer for reminding us how badly we wish we were there, and mostly we are eager to get back outside. It is still very hot.

The speaker's work is accomplished and professional, though it is not entirely appreciated in this crowd. It is, as they say, abstract, consisting mainly of broad black strokes on white background. Polite though his audience is, if they were made privy to this art vs. craft feud, they would take one look at his prints and side firmly with craft. If that's art, they might say, who needs it? Practice trumps theory. Earthy pragmatism is the norm. I guess, until tonight, I've never considered this a bad thing.

Too late for the sixties, I was a peace-and-love-struck kid who watched TV reruns of Woodstock sick with longing. When I was a teenager, my mom introduced me to the Sawdust Festival, a craft fair in Laguna Beach. I was wooed by the smell of sawdust and incense, homemade soaps. I ran my fingers over wood carvings and across woven wool, and gawked at the costumed jugglers on stilts, blacksmiths pounding on anvils. I was heady with the possibilities of creation, wandering among those funky makeshift booths, vine twisted and shingled, the unpainted grain of wood—pine, fir, redwood—everywhere. I bought the souvenir poster and swore to return each summer. The Sawdust Festival was awash in a kind of magic I could aspire to.

Besides, in a nerdly academic way, practice trumped theory in our house, too. My mom spent years completing her PhD, then abandoned the ivory tower to take a job at the community college, where she'd be allowed to teach Spanish conversation—a practical skill in Southern California if there ever was one— rather than, say, deconstruct Spanish literature from a Marxist/ feminist perspective.

Eventually, in the family tradition, I headed off to grad school, where I could fidget and roll my eyes for myself. In writing workshops, the idea of art seemed ethereal to me, something distant and out of reach. Craft sounded attainable, something that might be diagrammed or outlined or at least whipped into shape by a skillful editor. I ditched most of the accoutrements of grad school, the theoretical debates and the dark smoky bar angst, and spent most of my energy finagling ways to leave school early to go skiing. I graduated and raced back here to the woods, where I apprentice to a thousand crafty skills from chainsaw notching to pizza-dough making.

These days Mom is a regular visitor to this remote mountain valley. She's grown accustomed to this odd lifestyle of mine, maybe even proud. She is hardy and uncomplaining, but today we had sweltered back at the cabin long enough. This outing would, I thought, provide a little local color and some much-needed distraction. I may have been wrong. At the moment, my mom seems engrossed mainly in scratching the mosquito welts that cover her sandal-exposed ankles while her friends, a couple from California whom she met while teaching a semester in Spain, watch an osprey soar from its snag-top nest across the lake.

The artist unfurls one of his prints after another, and occasionally I recognize what you might call an essence, an exuberance of motion, say, or a sense of claustrophobia, but I have to admit it's a stretch. I feel as though I'm searching within myself the way I used to do in church to find meaning that I'm not sure is there. I can see others, the ones not chasing children or daydreaming or gazing at the sunset, straining in similar head-scratching ways.

Not that tonight's audience is exactly a portrait of cultural ignorance. The valley is full of people who, if pushed past the requisite humility, would call themselves artists. There is a Vietnam vet, now a full-time photographer, who specializes in capturing, besides the dramatic scenery, the aging faces of Native American elders. There are a handful of wood workers who use twisted limbs as table legs and chair arms, who take a cross section of a stump and polish it until the growth rings and the pith rise into surprising waves and ripples. There are ceramists and portraitists and a couple of hard-to-categorize tinkerers in whose work tools figure figuratively: rusted cogs and boilers are pieced together into, well, pieces. There are writers and musicians of considerable talent, and two or three art professors on leave or sabbatical, who don't often speak of their careers.

Tonight's speaker knows all this. He's kept a summer home in the valley for more than thirty years, and he knows almost everyone here. His unconscious prejudice isn't based on what people up here don't know, but on what we know, perhaps, too well. What I think the artist means, in part, when he implies that the art up here is mainly craft is that it centers on nature, and nature is already there, and, as many critics will tell you, making art about something that's already there is not as good as making it up.

Later, when I peruse the many online discussions that debate the subject, I'll find that one art educator offers the example of the cotton ball bunny: if you give children cotton balls and glue and paper, you give them the chance to make art; if you give them paper cut in the shape of a bunny, a pattern to follow, you give them a craft. That's the problem, critics seem to think: nature is our cotton ball bunny. They've got a point, I think. Not that we should avoid nature-as-subject. The danger lies in laziness, in the possibility that when interpreting nature, we fail to capture, well, its essence. On the other hand you can go overboard with this essence business.

Tonight's artist unwittingly offers one moment of hilarity when he holds up his interpretation of the forest at the edge of nightfall, a block print four or five feet tall that is almost entirely black.

"The problem here is obvious," he says, like a teacher asking a leading question.

The problem is not particularly obvious.

"It needs to be more black," he says.

The crowd rustles a bit and remains silent, the uncomfortable silence where nearly everyone is stifling a laugh and thinking the same thing: Gimme that thing and I'll make it more black for you.

From there, the evening disintegrates. Kids splash and squeal in the frigid lake water. Adults doze then startle awake. The artist passes around a glossy program from a recent show of his in San Francisco, and I briefly envy his life in the city, all that affirmation, the certainty it must bestow that what he is doing is not second tier. After all, as anyone in this audience will attest, artsy prejudice—real or perceived—has a lot to do with where you live.

When, at last, the talk is finished, I scan the crowd, then steer my guests out the back way. I dread running into Jean. I am uncomfortable with conflict, and I'm afraid she will corner me and make me take a side: art or craft.

Meanwhile, we are silent, my mom and her friends and I. This is the theme: If you can't say something nice, don't say anything at all. And the harshness of this unspoken judgment begins to bother me. After all, if a pro player showed up at the local ball field, the kids wouldn't condemn him if he were a tad snooty.

"Well," I say, "I respect anyone who stands in front of a group of people and says why they make art. I thought it was bold."

My mom's friends nod vaguely. They do not buy it. They have done the whole rigmarole: college, graduate school, art cinema club. This morning in the wee hours of early-summer dawn, he was in an armchair in the living room reading Heraclites. They have visited the great European art Meccas, but they have spent their careers teaching philosophy and psychology and sometimes how-to-write-a-complete-sentence in a community college on the smog-soaked fringes of L.A. They have an extremely low tolerance for pretension.

"I thought it was long," she says.

Here is the secret truth. The real reason I sympathize with tonight's speaker is not because he is the berated underdog, but because I agree with him. When I write, I want to make something that transcends the hows of everyday life, something of which people might say: the whole of that is so much more than the sum of its parts. But whenever I admit this to myself, that I aspire to that capital A, I feel like I do when I have to get dressed up. I stand awkwardly, exposed and out of fashion. I want to do this right, I think. I want to seem seamlessly one of them, whoever they are. Please. Please. Invariably I am a failure, a poser. An editor scoffs when I list a popular magazine alongside the literary journals where I've been published. That, she explains, is journalism. Not art. A story is rejected because, the photocopied slip explains, it is nonfiction. And nonfiction is not art. Though it can be craft. The echelon is absurd, and part of me thinks: Gimme that thing and I'll make it fiction for you.

What's worse, I worry, is that the ambition to create art is sometimes worse than silly. It's undemocratic. What you really want is to separate yourself from the crowd. Though I'm loath to admit it, I sometimes avoid writers' groups for just this reason: because I do not want to be chastened by the shortcomings of others. Maybe I don't have the patience it takes, the grace, to stand in the field awaiting a ball that will never, ever, be hit far enough to reach me. Maybe I cannot face the insecurity: am I as bad as that?

Mostly, I am scared. It takes such courage to sit at your desk looking out at your little world, then back in at your little self, culling meaning from it, and reworking the meaning, trying from such meager fodder to shape something transcendent. It is daunting, and despite my best efforts, wall gazing hogs the lion's share of my time.

And there on the wall in front of my desk hangs one of Jean's pieces. Called "First Snow," it captures the shock of light in a flat silvery world, the relief of it—winter at last!—and the threat, too, up here where winters are both long awaited and plain long. Slender leafless trees dominate the foreground. They are silhouetted against a dark river, silver sky, and a shock of white at the base. The white is speckled with beige, like patches of earth showing through. The fabric used on the mountainous ridge across the river has an unexpected horizontal weave that suggests the flatness of that cloud-defined season. And, sure, it means something to me because I live here, but we have scarcely a visitor who doesn't take note of it. Even people like my guests who live in snowless climes are drawn to the tension: equal parts relief and terror.

When the Dart does eventually pull up beside us, Jean is surprisingly unperturbed. She greets my mom kindly, as she always does, though she's met her only a couple of times before. And Mom thanks her for the evening.

Then Jean turns to me.

"What'd you think?"

"Well," I say, "I thought it was good."

Jean rolls her eyes and grins. Her face reads like a book. You are a coward, it says. Jean has fought her battles. She knows what she believes, and she knows how to deal with criticism.

"Well," she says, nodding toward her eighteen-year-old son—an aspiring writer and a master of the one-liner—sitting in the passenger seat of her Dart, "I guess he said it best."

"It was," he says, "ineffable."

Everyone laughs.

It's what we have to do, we who are relegated by geography or subject or medium or disposition to second tier. There is no point in decrying the injustice of it, anymore than there was a point in arguing in high school that we could be popular, that we should be, that it was pure whim and meanness that left us out. Better to shrug it off. So what if we're not popular? So what if what we make is not art? Who wants immortality anyway?

Who wants it? We all do, of course. All of us—painter, quilter, writer, whittler, teacher—wake up sometime in the night thinking the same thing: why do I do what I do? And maybe you find an answer. Maybe you don't. You do it anyway, and with equal parts relief and terror send it out to the world. Maybe someone will see an answer—an essence—the same one you intended or a different one. Maybe they won't. The answer is out there, but it is too impractical, too awesome or overwhelming or sacred to express in words. It is, perhaps, ineffable after all.

We wave farewell to Jean and walk to the car in fading daylight. As we begin to pull away, my mom points out a couple of dogs paddling along the shore. Whose dogs? And what are they doing out there? They might be far from home and in danger. It is a very large cold lake. I pull over to look more closely, and realize they are not dogs at all but a pair of river otters, playful and sleek, swimming in perfect unison, undulating toward the wide green mouth of the river, so I drive slowly, following the otters from a distance, memorizing the image, trying already to interpret it, while the otters—by instinct or inclination or pure whim—surface and dive, surface and dive.

The Woman Who Gardens with Bears

At certain times of the year, the orchard Laurie maintains becomes, as she puts it, a veritable Slip-and-Slide. The local black bears that gorge themselves on apples for several hours a day leave enough scat in sloppy mounds that you can't take three steps without landing in it. It's slippery when it was fresh in August, and slipperier in March when the snow melts and the preserved mounds, hundreds of them over four acres, reappear sporting a furry mold. Laurie not only has to watch her step, she has to watch her balance.

If it's an unusual hazard, hers is an unusual job.

The historic Buckner Orchard—three hundred aging apple trees preserved for posterity—is set in the ox-bow of a wild mountain river running fast and glacial blue at the base of granite cliffs rising steep. The scenery is stunning, the trees picturesque, the apples organically grown and free to any picker. But Laurie never intended to become an orchardist. It happened, more or less, by accident.

The saga is a long one. The National Park Service acquired the orchard in 1970 from the local postmaster, Harry Buckner, who could no longer keep up the operation. When Phil and Wendy Garfoot arrived the next year, the trees were unpruned and gangly, the irrigation ditches clogged, the grass tall, the garden weedy, but they fell in love with the place anyway. They settled in the old homestead, raised two kids and several loyal dogs. They hosted Mother's Day picnics and graduations, summer bonfires and square dances, even weddings, and in between—not to mention Phil's full-time job working on trail crew—they pruned and watered and mowed. But they couldn't do all the work. Volunteers helped out, and contracts were sometimes awarded, but care was inconsistent. The park would hire someone one summer, but not the next.

That changed, by happenstance, in the early 1990s, at exactly the same time Laurie lost her trail crew job in a complicated game of seasonal job roulette. She applied for the orchard job, she got it, and over time, she came to love it: the gnarly scabby-barked trees, the shovel-alone independence, even the challenges. Which came in spades.

The ditches, to start with. Miles of open ditches—*rills*, they're called—drew snowmelt down from the peaks, over a waterfall, under a small road bridge, through a short wooden flume, and eventually between the rows of trees, soaking the roots at the drip line. Or at least that was the idea. The ditches were clogged with silt and gravel, with cottonwood shoots and blackberry vines and Oregon grape roots thick as sisal rope. Laurie picked and shoveled the gravel and chopped the roots, then ran a weedeater until her hands vibrated numb and water ran free.

The water ran free, but it couldn't reach the end of the rills. Orchard grass carpeted the sandy loam like a too-effective trade embargo. Laurie tried breaking the six-inch-deep roots with a shovel. No go. Chopping with a Pulaski worked better but was too slow. Finally, she used a backhoe bucket to peel back the sod and make way for the water and the spread of aggressive weeds—knapweed, rush skeletonweed, toadflax, salsify—some of which she tried to battle. Since the orchard was organic, herbicides were out. Ditto for pesticides.

And there were pests aplenty: biting formica ants, wood-drilling flickers, defoliating red-humped caterpillars, and aphids—sticky, green, rosy, and omnipresent. Bigger pests, too: deer standing on their hind legs to eat low-hanging leaves

("Look," Laurie liked to tell whoever would listen, "they're evolving into kangaroos"), elk gnawing bark from the limbs down (even as mice gnawed from the ground up), girdling the trunks, mid-summer tourists coming out of the woods from every direction.

The job was an intricate balancing act, and, on balance, the act worked. Laurie sprayed soapy water on aphids, and she pruned tent caterpillar nests or burned them with a propane torch. She tossed the one-year-old whips from her summer pruning to the deer. She sicced Garfoots' dog, Yoda, on the mice—six in one day—and watched a raven chase the dog away. Everything in the orchard lived in tenuous harmony. With one exception.

The bears, save the poop, were hard to see. A branch swayed on a windless day. A green apple thunked to the ground. Finally you'd spot them wobbling on the twiggiest limbs, raking through leaves with their claws, lunging toward an apple, mouth-first, knocking dozens to the ground in the process, then lunging again. "They're wasteful," Wally Winkel always said, as if that were the worst part of the quandary: that the bears didn't clean their plates. Then the branch—or an entire trunk—would splinter or peel away and dangle grotesquely. The bear would stumble off like a drunkard, while the tree, often enough, would not recover. Though sometimes it did. Occasionally a bear-mauled trunk stripped entirely of limbs would grow a thick bush of suckers on top like a well-worn upside-down broom. Not good form. But at least it survived.

As did the bears.

Make no mistake. The bears needed no sympathy. They didn't need the orchard to survive anymore than humans did. There was plenty for them to eat in the hills—huckleberries, saskatoons, kinnickkinnick, mountain ash. Lots and lots of ants. But the bears preferred the orchard. Apples, after all, are a lot bigger than ants. The bears liked it there, and Laurie liked it too, so that first season she put up with them.

During the second season, the number increased. Some people said six. Some counted eight. Some claimed as many as thirteen black bears frequented the orchard. An especially large male slept, day after day, in a ponderosa next to where Laurie parked her bike, his body draped over a beefy limb fifty feet up. Visitors stepped off the tour bus and walked right under him.

"Have you seen any bears?" they asked.

Laurie never let on that one lounged right overhead. She looked forward to the day when scat would splat and the secret would be out.

One hot day in August, I brought Laurie lunch. She'd been digging up stumps with the backhoe, and she shut it off to sit with me for a while in the shade. Shortly after we sat, we spotted a sow and a cub wandering, wet and dreamy, like a couple of love-struck characters in a TV mini drama. They had swum the river and they were following their noses, as bears are always doing, but they looked lost, purposeless, as they stumbled from the frothy river through a dry pasture and into Shangri La, an apple orchard, three hundred trees of nearly ripe fruit. The sow looked as though she'd found the mother lode and wasted no time clambering into a tree and knocking bucketloads of apples to the ground.

I laughed.

Laurie scowled.

We looked around for the cub, but he seemed to have disappeared, so Laurie gulped the last of her coffee.

"Thanks for the visit. I gotta get back to work," she said.

We walked together through tall grass and a swarm of black flies that glommed onto Laurie, spinning circles around her head, and we headed toward the big ponderosa where I'd parked my bike next to hers. As we passed the backhoe, we saw the cub at last, curled in a ball in the bucket, warming itself in the sun.

"You have to admit he's awfully cute," I said.

Laurie just shook her head.

I looked up at the big male sleeping on the overhead limb and pedaled away.

The problem was getting out of hand. Bears dominated conversations throughout the valley. One afternoon our friend Chad, a Texan and a West Point grad, came upon a sow lazing on the front porch of his seasonal rental cabin beside a shredded screen door. Inside two cubs stood on their tiptoes on the white Formica counter and reached up to topple bags of pancake mix and dried hummus out of the cabinets. Chad was neither scared nor amused. He left the sow oblivious on the porch and raced in the back door with a club-like maple limb to chase the mewing cubs back through the shaggy screen into the hot sun.

His housemate was appalled.

"Don't you want your future grandkids to see a bear?" she asked.

"Not in their kitchen," Chad answered.

Historically, bears in the orchard were shot. Even now shooting them was not entirely out of the question. Hunting was legal almost everywhere in the valley—except the orchard. Maybe that was because of the close proximity to homes. More likely it was because it would not be fair to get the bears addicted to apples, then kill them.

But that's sometimes what happened anyway. The bears got used to humans in the orchard then moved on to nearby houses where they ravaged gardens and sniffed out garbage, and the cubs even sneaked through cat doors. When eventually their preference for human food made them too daring and foolhardy, often enough they were shot by homeowners who didn't need a permit to defend person or property. And many believed the problem started in the orchard. Solutions abounded—a fence for one thing—but that was a difficult suggestion to stomach. The orchard had become a place where people expected to see wildlife.

"Have you seen any bears?" a new ranger asked Laurie, feigning interest in helping her chase them away.

Laurie began to explain her idea to fence them out, and he interrupted: "But my kids sure love seeing them."

Chad, for his part, didn't worry much about to-fence or not-to-fence. He'd learned to use a rifle back at West Point, and he was at wit's end. With a little prodding from Laurie and me, he bought a bear tag—since he wasn't a homeowner, he needed one—and borrowed our pickup. It did not take long before the big male that slept in the ponderosa ventured out in search of water or newly arrived Kokanee salmon and passed outside the orchard boundary, where Chad lay in wait. When Chad returned the pickup to us, he was excited. The bear, he figured, had weighed over three hundred pounds. He planned to have a rug made for his dad back in San Antonio.

"Do you want to come over for dinner and try the backstrap? Best meat you'll ever taste."

"Sure," I said. "Sure."

But Laurie wasn't looking at him. She was staring at the two-by-eight tailgate board now stained with blood, and she kept staring in silence as Chad pedaled away on his bike to go finish the butchering. I knew what was up: blood on our tailgate meant blood on our hands, a regular couple of Lady Macbeths we were. As much as she wanted those bears gone, Laurie couldn't shake the unease.

The bears continued to wreak havoc in the orchard, swinging from branches, sauntering across the rills, posing, it seemed, for photographs each time the tour bus pulled in. Visitors flocked in, hoping to see a bear, and Laurie dodged them, recognizing that have-you-seen look on their faces from afar. She considered putting up a sign that read: Welcome to the Petting Zoo.

☙

Years passed, and though the job was seasonal and offered little security, Laurie stayed at it. She pruned and grafted; she burned the ditches with propane and propped limbs for the snow. She worked when the temperature topped one hundred and the bugs hovered like the plague. She kept a plastic hobby horse in the orchard—a local kindergartener named it "Gallop" a few years back—and moved it occasionally from treetop to treetop, and sometimes, for fun, she wore a gaudy colored housecoat while driving the tractor mower. Each year for a dozen, Phil and I joined her on the eve of the first snow to spread seven tons of chicken manure, purchased downlake and barged uplake, under the drip line of the trees. ("This is one chicken shit outfit we work for," Phil joked year after year.) We worked fast, trying to get it spread—off the pallets and out of plastic bags—before the bears got to it, clawing the bags apart, dragging them around, leaving the orchard looking like a frat house on Saturday morning. We'd light a bonfire and work until after dark, and Laurie would grow more animated as the day went on, tossing wet cottonwood rounds onto the fire, standing long in the skittering sparks.

"She's kind of unpredictable, isn't she?" Phil said. He shook his head with unbridled admiration. "She's a little bit crazy."

Each year her body wore down a notch: her hands, her shoulders, her neck, her knees. Each year an average of nine tree trunks collapsed. Most years a bear or two got killed. More than once, it was a sow with cubs. The bears moved slowly, though not methodically. They were haphazard, distracted by whatever came their way, and for all their ferocious image, most often they seem surprised by humans. Even Laurie, day after day. They gave her that look: what are *you* doing here?

Laurie yelled and threw rocks and used a slingshot. With help from bear biologists, the Park Service adopted a bear-shepherding program, and Laurie took to hazing them with a high-powered shotgun with rubber bullets, beanbags, and firecrackers or sometimes by trapping them and harassing them on site. The herding strategy worked at keeping the bears out during the daytime and disappointed a lot of gawkers and maybe saved a bear's life or two. But it didn't save the apples since the bears did their work at night. For several years there were nearly no apples left.

"How is the apple crop looking, Laurie?" locals asked.

"What do you do with all the apples?" visitors asked.

Laurie dreaded the answer she'd have to give: "The bears will get most of them."

She dreaded even more the question that so often came next: "Oh, have you seen any bears?"

Eventually, a fence section was approved. Laurie built it: cutting poles and peeling them, digging holes with a tractor auger, reeling out the concrete mesh, then electric wire. When the section was complete, hooked up to solar panels, and electrified, with some sadness and some relief, she shut the gate and waited to see what would happen. It worked. The bears stayed out. The trees, in that section at least, were safe.

It's hard sometimes to remember how bad it was. Each year in August when the bears arrived, Laurie hardly slept. And I didn't know what to do to help. One year, I bought an inflatable kayak, hoping that floating the river on the weekends might distract her. And it did, a little, until one day in September.

We were driving home from the orchard watching autumn sunlight slip behind yellow larches on the ridgetops and river water ripple—running too low this year—when suddenly, near our driveway, a wiggly-rumped bear appeared, coming toward us on the dusty road.

"What's up with him, you think? Shouldn't he be down at the orchard gorging himself?"

"Probably just curious, checking out the neighborhood. He's pretty cute, don't you think?"

"What?" After all those years of fretting and complaining, how could she say such a thing?

"You have to admit that little guy is cute," she said.

We'd spooked him with our pickup and he scampered downvalley behind us. In the rearview mirror I watched his haunches rolling like shoulders shrugging in a heavy coat.

"I guess," I said.

We pulled into the driveway beside the place where our new blue boat sat under a scraggly fir, ready and waiting for the weekend, but looking a little lopsided, one whole side deflated, entirely flat. I hopped out to take a closer look and found toothmarks galore, still wet with slobber. The little bear had been curious all right: there were twenty-six rips and tears in all.

"Still think he's cute?" I asked.

"Yeah," Laurie said. "I do."

In a few short weeks, the orchard would collect the sinking cold air, the first place in the valley to freeze hard. The few remaining apples would be nabbed, and the insatiable bears would wade out onto sand bars to gorge on spawned-out salmon, while Laurie worked alone, preparing the trees for winter, cold fingers fumbling with props and twine, anxious to be laid off. Then the bears would sleep hard in their secret dens, having waited for the late-arriving snow to cover their tracks, while Laurie sat at the kitchen table peeling apple bark from sawed-off limbs to use as door handles or coat hooks. Eventually, before spring, it would fall on her to patch the twenty-six holes in the heavy rubber kayak. I wouldn't have the patience. I don't know anyone else who would.

Saw Chips in My Bra

At the bakery in Stehekin, preteen boys stand apron clad at the sink. After this summer, or a couple more, they will be driving dump trucks, saddling horses, haying the fields, maybe eventually heading off to college. For now they are indoors, wiping sweat from their foreheads with an elbow, rubber-gloved hands slick with soap, while the preteen girls are out having a last hurrah: jumping from the dock to the lake, riding horses, striding—fists in pockets—through the woods. The boys stand still over steamy pots, their bangs plastered to acned foreheads. Everyone who stops in for a cinnamon roll or a loaf of multi-grain nods and grins approvingly at the boys: how *cute* they are!

One night when I was twelve, Mr. Frazier across the street was edging his lawn. Mr. Frazier was always edging his lawn after dinner. That, or shearing the hedge or poking a screwdriver into a sprinkler head or readjusting the American flag on his lamppost out front. Me, I was shooting baskets. That or throwing a tennis ball at a chalk-marked strike zone or slamming tennis balls against the garage door. It was a typical night on Burnside Court except that night Mr. Frazier decided to talk to me.

"One of these days you're gonna outgrow that," he hollered over to me.

Outgrow what? I wondered. I was stumped.

He tipped his crew cut toward the backboard affixed to our house gutter in a gesture full of derision, one he might reserve for unruly teenagers or unkempt lawns. "Boys' stuff," he said.

I shrugged and turned away.

I knew that my sprinkler-soaked world, my cul-de-sac of safe existence, had just sprung a slow leak. I took three long strides toward the juniper hedge, cupped the ball in one hand, and sent a hook shot sailing from twelve feet out. Mr. Frazier shook his head and returned to edging. Me, I watched the ball sail high. I'd practiced that shot a million times, so I knew it would swish through the net. And it did. I also knew this: Mr. Frazier was wrong.

One early summer day, Phil and I were logging out to Purple Pass on a trail that gains six thousand feet of elevation steadily, mercilessly, over seven miles. I'd been working for him on the trail crew by then for a decade, and I'd long since convinced him that I could run the chainsaw. Now I hiked with the twenty-inch bar lying across a scrap of horse blanket on my right shoulder. Gas leaked from the tank onto my pack and made me feel nostalgic. I couldn't help it. Over time, the pleasures and discomforts of trail work had mixed together—the smell of saw gas and pine needles, the taste of mountain water in a dirty plastic bottle, the familiar annoyance of saw chips in my bra. So I sawed, and Phil cleared the logs and debris off the trail in my wake—"swamping," we call it—and the trail was steep, and we were both out of shape. He huffed and panted as he told me a story about his former high school baseball coach, a man he admired, who was embroiled in a controversy.

I couldn't follow the details. The story was complicated, and Phil was out of breath, and as we hiked, he grew angrier. But I caught the gist: the softball team at the university where Phil's coach now worked had been getting more money than the baseball team, and Phil's coach had thrown a public fit, and now, because of the fit, his job was threatened. Softball, in short, was undercutting baseball and at fault, Phil claimed, was Title IX, the girls' sports legislation. He'd read it in *Baseball Weekly.*

"I don't have anything against girls' sports," he said, "But softball is not a major sport, and baseball is."

I should have let it go. One of the unspoken roles of women on all-male crews is to deflect attention always off ourselves, off our gender. If men had had to face the accusatory glare of a figurative Mr. Frazier, they'd deflect, too. Like the boys at the sink at the bakery who can sense all eyes upon them—*how cute!*—and want to finish their shift and get the hell out of there, we're experts at ducking out. I would normally have been happy to deflect attention off Title IX to a more benign topic, like which sport is more major: baseball or fencing? baseball or soccer? Except for the obvious.

"But Phil, girls aren't allowed to play baseball."

I tried to explain Title IX, how it's about equal rights, how it's empowering for high school girls. Like his daughter. Like me. I tried to appeal to the side of him that made arguments about the moral rightness of sports: sports as metaphor, sports as life-preparation arguments. But we were beyond that.

"Softball is not a major sport," he said more loudly.

"Girls aren't allowed to play baseball!" I cried, incredulous, and now very angry.

Phil always said: never show weakness. The look on his face said he was digging in. There'd be no discussion.

"Softball," he said, "is not a major sport."

Most Friday nights in Stehekin, some guys—and a few of us girls—sit around a smoky campfire at Wally's drinking canned beer, some sipping, some swilling. Friday Night Club, Wally calls it. Conversation zips from the governor (the men categorically oppose her) to mason bees (Wally favors them, cultivates them, obsesses over them) to the stock market. Wally is full of financial advice.

"Bonds. Put it all in bonds." He nods conspiratorially and waits for a response.

"OK," I say.

Later, after the beer takes hold, the stories begin, and we can feel them coming: the time he dumped the loader in Rainbow Creek, the time he had to snowshoe to the powerhouse after midnight in a blizzard, then further back in time, to his youth. Laurie gestures with a swift karate chop across her long hair, and we know which childhood story is on deck: how Wally rode from Florida to Michigan in the 1940s on a train.

He always starts the story the same way. He dips his head boyishly and makes his own karate chop motion beside his ear so that we can't help but picture Little Lord Fauntleroy.

"Our hair was long," he says.

We know the rest of the story by heart, every detail about how his father was a businessman who spent most of his time in the lounge car and how Wally and his brothers sat still, chastened, and watched the dramatic scenery unfold. We've heard it a thousand times, and we listen just the same.

Wally is not from here. He's remade himself, and these stories are part of the remaking. In the early 1950s, when Wally was a new arrival on Lake Chelan, each Friday a handful of mountain men, weary of solitude, used to come down the trail to nearby Lucerne to drink and shoot the breeze. Wally must have revered those men something fierce because he's kept the tradition alive for fifty years. Each Friday he starts a fire in a rock-lined pit. He sits on a metal folding chair beside a bucket of warm Budweiser and waits to hold court, which he does in a strange barely decipherable grumble. Sometimes you can't understand a word Wally says. Other times, he's clear as glass. Timbre, inflection, enunciation, even punctuation: perfect.

Once a friend explained it to me. Apparently one of the regulars at the original Friday Night Club, a real live mountain man, had a hair lip. Wally's grumble honors his memory. And that's how almost everything is with Wally. He pretends to be gruff, but he's really soft. He pretends to be a mountain man, but he has not, in the years I've known him, ever left the valley floor. He also pretends to dislike women.

"Witches," he likes to say when we show up. "Here come the witches."

He says this with the determined scowl of a delighted four-year-old.

Once, a few years back, Wally announced that Friday Night Club should only be for men.

"We need time for boy talk," he growled.

In protest, a group of women planned an unofficial sort of Ladies' Night. We showed up wearing dresses, and we talked a couple of guys into cross-dressing as well: skirts fashioned from tablecloths, earrings from fishing lures. A crowd gathered by the campfire, the largest ever, twelve people, maybe fifteen. Usually shy men in work boots, now surprisingly giddy, donned plastic sequined glasses for photos. Women in dresses passed around a tube of gaudy lipstick then came forward one at a time to smooch Wally on the cheek.

"Witches," he growled and leaned forward, over and over, to receive the next kiss until his face was splotchy red.

These days at Friday Night Club it seems ridiculous that being allowed to attend was ever such a big deal because, frankly, it can be awfully boring. Conversation starts, then peters. Wally's dog Molly, a scruffy mutt covered in forest litter—twigs, needles, moss—that sticks to her unwashed fur like a nature collage, pants at his feet and paws her ears. Mites, probably. His cat, Killer, a sweet-natured calico, prowls in search of a lap. Birds making their twilight racket are the rowdiest attendees.

"Gonna be sad when the birds finish nesting for the spring," Phil says.

Wally nods. "Ah, them robins have been nesting twice in recent years. They'll be back." This, the extent of the banter.

More silence.

"You got bees at your place?"

Not the bees, we all think. Please not the damned bees again.

"Yeah I do," someone offers. "They're nesting in the recessed screw holes on my weedeater. Didn't you say the holes have to be 9/16ths? These aren't 9/16ths." He's ribbing now, trying to step things up a notch, but Wally won't take the bait. He draws on his hand-rolled cigarette and stares into the woods, then flips the bird.

"Nine-sixteenths. I told you."

Wally's older brother, a retired orchardist from downlake, cradles Killer in his lap.

"You're spoiling her," Wally grumbles.

"Ah," his brother says, "you don't love her enough."

These are fighting words. Wally loves Molly and Killer plenty, too much probably. When he drops short notes in the mail occasionally—he'll never adopt the Internet—to thank us for a borrowed tool, say, or to decline an invitation to a party, he signs all three names: Wally, Molly, and Killer Cat. Wally's brother scratches Killer under the chin, and Killer purrs, and Wally glares at Killer like a two-timer. He takes a swig of Budweiser and a long drag off his cigarette.

All the older men—Wally, his brother, Phil—sit on cushions now, the trapezoid rocking chair type with strings. We pretend not to notice.

On our way up Purple, I tried to explain to Phil how I had *believed* I could be a famous pitcher and how it felt to discover that I could not. Not so much discover, as admit. I wasn't blind. I knew women didn't play in the majors. I just liked to pretend that didn't mean they couldn't. Maybe they just hadn't tried hard enough. As we argued, I returned in my mind to Burnside Court, where as a kid I wrapped my fingers around the tennis ball hidden in my glove, perfecting my grip. I'd memorized the Dodgers lineup and listened to games with my transistor smashed tight to my sweaty ear. I'd known, back then, what I wanted. I wanted to pitch. I would be the next Bruce Sutter, the next Burt Houghton even, if anyone could teach me to throw a knuckleball with a dog-chewed tennis ball. I wound up and followed through, aiming for the chalk-marked strike zone on the garage door. I rehearsed post-game interviews aloud. And I doggedly ignored the truth: that I could never, ever, pitch in the majors.

As a kid I couldn't face bald-faced injustice. I still couldn't. I didn't care a whit about softball. What I really wanted to say was that I had *believed* I could be a trails worker. I'd even believed that one day I might take over Phil's job as foreman. It was still a real possibility, if I could just hang on a little longer. But something had snapped. I knew, like I had known that long-ago day with Mr. Frazier, that this conversation had snagged on something stringy like the inside of a baseball, less solid than it ought to be, and I was losing my footing—not on the trail, no, but in my deepest self—my grounding. I was also losing my temper.

"Women aren't allowed to play baseball," I said.

"Softball is not a major sport," Phil said.

I turned and walked fast, then faster, and in no time I was far ahead of him. When I came to a log across the trail, I cut it and rolled it down the switchbacks, a dangerous practice. If he wanted to play hard ball, he'd have to prove himself, and he could not keep up. He couldn't have kept up, truth be told, on the day of the season when he was in his best shape—he was over sixty, after all—though I knew I'd never again run ahead like that to prove anything. If I wanted to hang on, I knew what I'd have to do: I'd have to try, always, to wrap my mind around other perspectives, to be accepting and understanding and forgiving, or at least pretend to be. Maybe it's the way I'm made, the planet I'm from (Venus, it turns out, not Mars); mostly it was the way I was required to be. And of all the snaggy truths, this was the snaggiest: if I wanted to be one of the boys, I'd have to act my girliest.

Q

"If you really want to see her hike," Phil said one Friday night a few months later, "make her mad."

Then he laughed.

I didn't argue because I knew that this time the point of the story wasn't to annoy me but to lighten the mood.

Molly was dying, and Wally would not put her to sleep. He'd made her a bed by the fire, and he changed her diaper-like bedding every few hours, and he waited. For weeks. It was winter, so Friday Night Club had moved inside Wally's shop, a garage crammed full of ancient gadgets and parts, scraps of wire and used spark plugs, filters and belts, gear lube and ATF fluid, and on Fridays, warm Budweiser. Week after week we crowded under the 1974 Rainier Beer calendar of semi-naked girls waiting for Wally to feed the barrel stove more soggy cottonwood and avoiding the subject of the dying dog.

Now, as Phil's story ended, Wally brought the subject up himself.

"Molly gives me that look," he said and jutted his lower lip out in exaggerated sadness. "She's just not ready to go."

"You're doing the right thing, Wally," Phil said. "You're doing good."

A long awkward silence followed. I picked up an oil filter wrench from the shelf I'd been leaning against and fiddled with it in my lap. We were sad for when Molly would be gone—Molly with her ear mites and ratty fur, who panted too hot and close and needy. And we were sad for Wally without her. And, I think, we were sad for the unspoken future, when it would be Wally himself. How long could he stick it out up here alone, sick and dying, without family? And what about the rest of us? In some ways, it occurred to me as Wally shed some tears under the naked beer ladies, the lesson about gender in Stehekin is the same as the lesson about everything: never show weakness. It sounds like a tough guy maxim, but it comes with a generous dose of diaper-changing compassion, and has more to do with facing the truth than with blind stoicism.

After a while the awkwardness passed and we moved on to something new, the lousy weather forecast—more wet snow— then the lousy news from the Middle East.

Around ten, the evening coasted toward a stop. Wally dozed in his chair, waiting for us to leave so he could get into the house to watch his weekly opera show on satellite TV. Phil headed home. Laurie and I grabbed our coats and flashlights and stood.

"See you in church on Sunday. I'll take the collection plate," Wally mumbled from his half-sleep. He said this every week.

"OK," I said.

"Give you ten percent." His punchline.

"OK," I said again, and looked back at where he sat, his logging boots unlaced, his cigarette ashes creeping toward his chin.

Suddenly he jerked upright.

"Hey, girls. Girls."

"What, Wally?"

"Thanks for coming," he said. "Come again."

That night, as Laurie and I walked into the moonless dark, I knew several things. I knew that we would come to Wally's again, and that these friendships, oddly configured as they were—with Phil, with Wally—would outpace so many others, in length and depth. I knew that preteen boys would continue to line the sinks at the bakery, and girls would continue to work on trail crew. But not me. Not for much longer.

Spawning in Mud

The rain began the day I was laid off for the season. If the day had been clear and sunny, I would have busied myself with our unfinished woodshed, climbed up on the roof to tack nailers in place, say, or set mill slabs against the back to keep snow from sifting in. As if snow were a possibility. We'd been without a trace of precipitation for seven months, so long that it seemed, genuinely, like we'd never see storm clouds again. On trail crew, we'd stopped carrying jackets. At home, we'd stopped covering our tools. On that day, rain streamed down, silver and continuous as mercury, puddling around a tangle of extension cords in the dirt, while I sat indoors drinking coffee and watching it fall.

The truth is I hadn't just been laid off; I had *asked* to be laid off. The weight of that unfinished woodshed hung over me like the dense wildfire smoke that, by October, had barely begun to dissipate. For fifteen years Laurie and I had been building and building: at work on trails or in the orchard and more recently at home on our own cabin. By the time we started on the woodshed, we'd about had it. We'd managed to take little weekend stabs at the project; we'd poured footings and peeled poles. Then, inevitably, my back would go out. I'd lie on ice. I'd try to stretch. Then I'd go to work, where the satisfaction of unglorious labor was eroding. So I drained the gas from the chainsaws in the trails shop, and for the first time ever, I asked to be laid off early, ostensibly to work on the shed. Now there it sat, roofless, while it rained. And rained.

I stepped out the door barefoot and tried to coax the cat, Daisy, out past the jamb. Forget it. All that noise! All that water! Sometimes, during a summer thunderstorm, we might get an hour of raucous spattering, enough to draw streaks across dust-coated leaves of maple and thimbleberry. This time the deluge was for real. Greenness everywhere was rinsed shiny clean, fresh, and in a way foreign. I stood on the porch, and I felt like when I was a suburban kid in Southern California on the "It's A Small World" ride at Disneyland, floating into a rain forest where tinsel hangs from the ceiling and recorded rainfall competes with monkey howls and the squawking of tropical birds. I half-expected to hear a macaw, but I only heard pounding rain, and after a while, through the trees, I thought I could hear the river. No, I told myself. It couldn't be.

Though not officially designated as such, the Stehekin River is, more or less, wild. It is undammed and largely unmanipulated for the thirty miles between the glacier-fed headwaters and the place, a mile from the boat landing, where it spills into Lake Chelan. Because of that, and because of the steepness, closeness, and snowiness of the mountains that feed it, the water level fluctuates wildly. In spring, snowmelt from the mountains can bring regular flows of 5,000 cubic feet per second (CFS) or more. These numbers, themselves, were relatively new to us. A USGS gauge on the river reported the volume of water running—via satellite—at three-hour intervals to a Web site. Since Internet service arrived in the valley, the numbers had become a regular part of daily conversation. What's the river down to? By August the river drops below 500 CFS, and there it stays, usually, for most of the winter. Except when it floods. During that last big one, eight years before, the river had risen to 20,000 CFS, a ridiculous unheard-of number. A hundred-year flood, the experts had called it.

○

Laurie came home from work for lunch. Her clothes were soaked, and she needed to change. But she put that off.

"Come on," she said. "Let's go look at the river."

I was wearing shorts. I felt lethargic, spinny from too much caffeine, guilty for not working on the woodshed.

"Why?" I asked.

"The water's getting pretty high," she said. "It might flood."

Flood? I thought she'd lost her mind.

All summer the threat of a catastrophic wildfire had cast a pall over the valley. Ferns browned up and bowed over. Twigs snapped under Vibram soles, and we winced. I'd spent so much dread on wildfires that I'd forgotten completely about floods. Besides, after that hundred-year flood eight years back, didn't we have a ninety-two-year hiatus coming?

"Come on," she said.

She pointed to my boots in the corner, where I'd left them after my last day of trail work. I pulled them on, and we headed out. The extension cords in the yard were now completely submerged and barely visible. The earth had been too dry for too long, and now it would not accept water, but repelled it, dust-like, so that the whole forest floor was filling up like a series of plastic kiddy pools. Hydrophobic, people would say later: the soil had gone hydrophobic.

Laurie and I splashed on through. As we neared the river, the puddles began moving in rivulets that divided and spread like a crowd racing for their cars after a ball game. We stood on the bank with our camera and waved at schoolkids standing on the opposite bank. Laurie jumped up and down, mimicking a *bufadora*—one of those blowholes through which Pacific waves erupt on the Mexican coast—as water sprayed over the top of a log jam, like storm-driven surf. The kids mimicked her.

I stood still.

The air buzzed and roared with excitement, but I resisted. As a seasonal laborer on backcountry trail crews, I would have been free to give in to it. We cheered when trail bridges washed away; if it meant more work for us, that was fine. The river not only had more might than us, I figured back then, but more right, too. Once, when I worked in Canyonlands, a visitor had knocked at my door in the middle of the night to tell me about a rattlesnake she'd seen in the backcountry. Someone should do something about it, she said. The park belongs to the rattlesnakes, I said, and I shut the door. For many years I believed something similar about floods. The valley belongs to the river. The difference was that now that we'd settled down and bought land and built a home, we belonged to the valley too.

On our way back home, a familiar pickup slowed next to us.

"I think it's gonna get wild," the driver said.

After he drove off, we walked in silence. If we were a little late catching the hint, we did have an excuse. Experts had explained November floods to us this way: snow comes too early and then melts too fast when the freezing level rises and rain sets in. There's a name for that: a rain-on-snow event. This time there was precious little snow in the mountains, and the rain had only begun the night before. I'd even checked the Web site mid-morning: only 6,000 CFS. The fact that the pickup driver—who had lived his whole life in Stehekin and didn't need expert analysis or Internet numbers to recognize a flood—said it was going to get wild was sobering.

We climbed the bank, twenty feet or so, to the slightly higher ground where we'd built our cabin—a wise decision that now seemed—and went inside to begin to fill water bottles, therm-oses, the bathtub even, preparing for the inevitable power outage. The river continued to rise. At dusk we ventured out one last time. I still wore shorts, and the fact that it was summer-clothes warm did not seem like a good omen. The water had already reached the bottom log of a vacation home across the road that sits on a three-foot-high foundation. By now, it seemed less like a river than the ocean. Swells formed and curled over amongst the trees. A charging persistent roar grew louder and more sea-like by the minute. With all the displaced fish—would-be spawning salmon now adrift in the churn—it even smelled like the ocean.

Stehekin salmon are not what you might think. They're not mighty ocean-farers, but smaller wiry landlocked sockeyes called Kokanees, who make a comparatively short trip from the lake upstream to lay eggs. Through most of September and October, while portaging our inflatable kayak through the shallows, Laurie and I, as a rule, try not to stir up too much mud in the shallows of the river, try to give them a little personal space. But this was late October, which is pretty late in their game. These hangers-on—eggs laid, business done, skin flapping, color fading—had apparently hung on just for this one last wild ride. They didn't stand a chance.

So the flood smelled like the ocean. And, Laurie noted, like a lumber mill. And she was right. All those logs—roots and limbs, freshly torn, needles dangling, careening past or jamming up, straining in the current, then breaking loose, cannon-shot—could have built a thousand homes.

Back at home, the power went out, so we sat in the dark, the room flickering orange from woodstove fire, and we listened to a handheld radio. Some people still had power, and they were watching the numbers on the Internet. Up to 12,000, they reported. Still rising.

"Twenty thousand," Laurie said. "I'll bet it's as big as '96!"

"No way," I said. "Sixteen five max."

This is not so bad, I thought. Everyone is over-reacting. We went to sleep listening to the roar.

In the morning, when the highest high water seemed to have passed, we made drip coffee, one cup at a very slow time, on a single-burner backpacker stove, before stepping out to check on a couple in their sixties, part-time residents, who had likely never seen such an event—had any of us, really?—and who may not have thought to move to higher ground.

"They can't be at home," I argued. "They wouldn't have stayed."

Laurie ignored me and charged ahead through the sopping brush.

From a distance, we saw a wisp of smoke.

"Ahoy, mates," the neighbors called.

The couple stood on their top step barefoot, checking out the mud-streak level on the side of the cabin; the river had been a quarter inch from barging in. They had been isolated, a half mile from anyone, without even a radio. Nevertheless, they were in good spirits. They posed for photos, and wandered out into the muck. I was impressed. These folks were used to risk. The barefoot man had spent years flying hang gliders and once survived a hot air balloon crash. His wife frequently traveled alone in South America. No one was going to get too wound up. The attitude, at first, was astonishingly nonchalant: Oh, that.

Back at the house, people began to trickle in, the intrepid out to survey the damage, others trying to get home after having bailed out. We served coffee and apple quarters and peanut butter, anything that did not require cooking or opening the refrigerator, since the power was off and seemed likely to stay that way. The damage was hard to assess because water still ran down the road, as far as anyone could see, and in many places braided out through the woods. The silt in many places had the consistency of pudding. Many homes had taken in water. And one house, the postmaster's, had been completely lost. Last anyone saw, it sat teetering over the froth, splintering slowly away. Friends came and went. Dishes piled up. The sun broke through the clouds. Steam rose. And, like an undercurrent, the blaming began.

We should have dredged the channel years ago, some people said. We should have hardened the banks. If only the river hadn't been dredged in the seventies, others said. If only people hadn't built where they did. I tried to steer clear. I wondered: is it possible that no matter what we did, or didn't do, we would face this? I didn't dare say so. Some people just needed to vent. They needed to feel that someone had done something wrong and that there was something someone should do to make it right.

Meanwhile, everywhere, children and dogs were collecting salmon. The kids placed them gingerly back in the muddy flow. The dogs carried them to their monstrous haystack mound in the summertime ball field. The Kokanee, it turns out, aren't native to Lake Chelan—they were introduced by the state in the 1910s—but scientists concede that they are now "natural," an official designation, since they've been going back and forth from the big lake to the small creeks on four-year cycles for nearly a hundred years. The population is stable, they say, and even a flood can't hurt it much. If the eggs, this time, don't make it, there will be another wave of pilgrims next year, on a different cycle. Migration is hard-wired for species survival, even if it can be a little harsh on individuals. Still it was hard, in the aftermath of the flood, not to feel some sympathy for these undersized fish who had worked so damned hard, following an instinct that's so often characterized as nature metaphor and comfort—sex and birth and home—only to end up toothmarked in a mass grave.

"Don't you want to come back to work?" Phil asked me one day. "Help out with the clean up?"

"No," I answered. It was just the truth.

Instead, I stayed at home sweeping, washing coffee mugs with water saved in the bathtub and heated on the woodstove, loads of them. The power outage had lasted nearly a week, and the end was nowhere in sight. I wished that I could work on the woodshed, but knew better than to go hammering away while others tried to piece their lives back together. I could have prepared for a wild Halloween party we had planned, but anymore I wasn't all that enamored with wildness.

"Do you want to come back to work?" Phil asked again the next day. "Take a helicopter ride to survey the damage upvalley?"

"Yes," I said. For clean up, no. For a helicopter ride, yes. I had no shame.

They'd fly Phil and me twenty-three miles to the end of the road, they said, and we'd walk back, taking pictures and notes, making suggestions for repairs. Even though I'd heard the final number—26,000 CFS!— as rotors began to spin, I was still thinking: this is a boondoggle, a free ride. The reports of the damage, I was sure, had been greatly exaggerated. We rose into the turbulent air over our thin slice of the universe, so striking at this time of year, a Crayola box of colors: dogwoods pink, cottonwoods yellow, and maples red, and the river, like a child's silver marker slash, haphazard, uninhibited, flashing amidst the broken-off trees. So many trees lying every which way. Like a dumped box of matches. Like pick-up sticks strewn across the Sahara, huge dunes of beachy clean sand.

Soon we were over the uninhabited part of the valley, the part where no one had yet been, and the pilot pointed out a section of road that might be difficult to negotiate on foot. Huh? Where was the road? We couldn't tell, even though I'd driven that road a thousand times, and Phil had driven it ten thousand times. In fifteen minutes in the air, I remembered what I'd been trying to forget for a week: that I needed this the way I need open-caskets at funerals. Until I see things firsthand, I just don't get it. The ship bounced and skipped on the winds of an incoming storm. I fought nausea, and still, I was glad as hell to be there.

Even from the air I knew that, by the next summer, when I'd have to hoof it around the missing road chunks and repair the damaged trails, it would no longer seem awesome, this flood. It would no longer be, simply, what happens. It would be, simply, a pain in the ass. But like the earliest, easiest moments of love, that first view was effused with pure unadulterated wonder. No longer: Oh, that. Now breath sucked sharp: Oh!

At last, the pilot brought us down to earth on a river bar. Phil and I walked the former road for the rest of the day, balancing on trees lying across trees, crawling under them and clambering over them. And we called out to each other. Would you look at this? We were back in the realm of particulars, notebook and camera, getting our bearings, settling in, walking, walking, walking. We skirted landslides and descended toward a long stretch of former-road beside the river, constructed by the CCC in the 1930s, now washed to bedrock, blasted granite worn table-top smooth, sloping toward the churn. One-inch-diameter iron anchors that used to hold rock in place, bent over like wet grass. One small fir stood alone on a rock outcropping with a five-foot-long skirt of twisted roots and caught brush like the draped fabric beneath a Christmas tree. How it had survived, I could not imagine. Drizzle started, then picked up, and I shot more pictures until finally we reached the spot that the pilot had pointed out from the air. A sheer cliff vanished in the froth. No way to cross.

We climbed up the cutbank and onto the rocky slope. We slipped on moss, and held onto roots—vegetable belay!—to pull ourselves further, up and up, and suddenly it became an adventure—no pictures to take up here, no figures to pencil-scrawl in the Rite-in-the-Rain notebook. We found an old backpack pump from a fire decades before, and knew, as we always knew, that we weren't the first to be here, just one more migrating wave. We sat on the high point and gazed across at the unchanged mountainsides. We could no longer hear the river roar or smell the fish, only the leaf decay musk of late fall, a familiar soothing smell, like a salve, like an ending. Together we sipped the last of our tea as rain soaked heavy into wool.

Back at home, the woodshed roof went on in a day. Mops were hung out to dry in a welcome stretch of slanty sun days. And a final decision was made: the party would go on. We strung colored lights around the house and the new empty woodshed outside, built a barrel fire in the woodshed and a bonfire in the woods. Then the partygoers trickled in: no fewer than five Vikings, a spotted cow with a rubber glove udder, and one scantily clad hussy with a black nose and a bushy tail calling herself a "Whorey Marmot." Darkness fell and the music grew loud, and the temperature dropped to single digits. A gorilla sipped beer through a curly straw up one nostril and eventually, predictably—he couldn't help it!—popped the cow's udder. Dancing and fires raged until two in the morning, then three. The Whorey Marmot had to recostume. Too many propositions.

On the morning-after, we gathered for breakfast—eggs and potatoes, fruit, and mimosas—then ventured out in pairs or small groups to see the floody sights. Laurie and I walked with a small crowd amongst the log jams and the sand traps, twisted fencing everywhere, and then to the summer homes near the former river banks. In one cabin, where the river had charged through one wall and out the other, a mounted deer head, cocked ajar, surveyed a scene of jumbled furniture, broken glassware, and fir limbs, looking as startled as the whole bewildered valley.

On the way home, we walked the former road eroded three feet deep just below our house.

"Don't you think they'll eventually move the road to high ground behind your house?" a neighbor asked.

I shrugged. Oh, that. "Sure," I said.

"What then?"

"Then we're screwed."

She nodded.

What else is there to say? After fifteen years on trail crews, not one major bridge I built is still standing. Erosion happens. Sometimes it happens fast. The corner post of our woodshed sits precariously on the edge of the bench, where we chose to put it—cleverly, we thought—so that snow would shed more effectively down the bank. Now it was clear: the woodshed would go first and later, just maybe, the cornerstone of the house. Down, down, down. Or, if not that, next fire season, the whole valley might burn up. No way to know. Uncertainty is part of the bargain.

News reports make a big deal about the community spirit that arises in the wake of disaster. People donate clothes and food or slow-brewed cups of coffee. They show their best side, then go home. But there's a deeper, more subtle way that natural disasters draw people together, day after day, living in the mutual terror and awe. Nature does win after all. There's nothing we can do, but head out, shoulders shrugging, shovel in hand. That, and wait.

For several months, everyone waited, one eye on the thermometer, one on the snow up high, to see what might happen next. Not much. Spring remained cold. Snow melted lazily. The Internet river gauge rarely nosed over 2,000. Summer brought smoky skies. On trail crew Phil and I and the crew chipped away at the flood damage, rebuilding bridge cribbing we'd rebuilt before. At home, on the weekends, Laurie and I entertained houseguests and lazed on river beaches, books in hand. Come September, a new batch of salmon began wriggling upriver, frisky as ever, eager to navigate the flood-shifted shallows in search of a little gravel in which to settle and lay a few eggs until, by October, they blanketed the river, slowly disintegrating, natural as the seasons changing, the leaves falling, browning up, layering into a thick fertile mat.

Defensible Space

A small crowd assembles outside a modest cabin, pushing wheelbarrows, carrying rakes and loppers, chainsaws and gas. The cabin, like most in this tiny mountain town, is tucked among trees: cedar, fir, pine, maple, dogwood, cottonwood. The crowd is anxious. Bob, the brand-new volunteer fire chief, straps on spurs and begins to climb a tall fir to remove low-hanging limbs. The rest of us buck downed wood and restack firewood, trying to create so-called defensible space, an area of two hundred feet or so around a house wherein burnable stuff is, for the most part, eliminated. We do this every Monday night at a different neighbor's home, but this week the task feels more urgent with an early-season wildfire burning just ten miles upvalley. Helicopters thwap overhead. Volunteers lean on pickups to debate firefighting tactics. I put in my ear plugs, pull the starter cord on a chainsaw, and begin to work. I'm a newly elected fire commissioner in a newly created rural fire district, and I don't have a thing to say.

When I was a kid in Southern California, each October, the sky turned orange and the sickly smell of smoke replaced the sickly smell of smog, and on TV, red garlands of flames snaked down brown suede hills. Weeping women stepped in flip-flops through the charred remains of mountain cabins. Bazillion-dollar homes in Malibu tottered uncertainly, silhouetted black against roiling flames, then fell and slid toward the sea. For an eight-year-old like me, cross-legged on the shag rug, there should've been terror in it, except that it was a regular occurrence, as predictable as

137

the World Series or Wimbledon. With a shrug, I thought: Gawd, how dumb! Those people should move away!

Today, outside the cabin in Stehekin, the sky turns dirty yellow as overcooked squash. It happens every year. Anymore, the Big One comes annually or semi-annually. Fifteen years ago, while working seasonally for the National Park Service, I sat in an office and mapped the fire history of this region. In a hundred years, there'd been fewer than ten fires that had grown over one hundred acres. Since that time—in fifteen short years—we've watched fires in the surrounding wilderness areas burn five thousand acres, then fifty thousand. The sheriff shows up on our doorstep regularly to deliver evacuation notices that stack up like junk mail next to the woodstove.

There are plenty of reasons why the situation has gotten so dire. Most people agree that a hundred years of fire suppression created the lousy forest conditions—trees crowded too tight, disease and pest plagued—and global warming means hot dry summers getting hotter and drier. Other people, including some of my neighbors, argue that at least part of the problem is the paralysis created by firefighter safety regulations that are strict and getting stricter. They bristle at the appearance each summer of out-of-state overhead teams—pre-assembled emergency-response teams—that often lumber into town far too late, long after the flames are up and running, to fight fire like a United Nations peacekeeping force: visible everywhere, active nowhere. It's all true. I've seen it. I cannot argue with anyone. Anymore, I can't even see the point in arguing.

So I'm running a chainsaw instead.

I walk through the woods felling small-diameter trees, scraggly and sun deprived, removing these small trees that might carry fire into the canopy while leaving the rest to keep things shaded and cool when the Big One comes. Other volunteers buck the downed trees into firewood or rake duff away from the cabin or drag brush to piles that we'll burn in fall, once the rains begin and the threat of flood, rather than fire, dominates.

Eventually, I shut off the saw, and a neighbor calls out to me.

"What's the plan up there on the hill? You going to briefing in the morning?"

"I think it's John's turn," I say.

"But what's going on? What's the strategy?"

I shrug, feeling cornered. Not for the first time, I think my little venture into politics has been a mistake.

"More of the same," I say.

He grimaces, nods, and tips a wheelbarrow on its front wheel, leaving a divot behind in the dirt.

I know why he's annoyed: it's hard to feel powerless when so much is at stake. I love this place. I love it blindly, indiscriminately, unconditionally, probably foolishly. I love it because the mountains rise steep and craggy, and the forest holds silence like a blessing, and the river runs fast and blue, and when you grew up near Los Angeles, there is no feeling in the world like arriving in such a place. Like finding a Get Out of Jail Free card in your back pocket. Like venturing cat-like onto the front porch after a long cold winter, squinting in the sun, sniffing the spring air. Really? Really?

So we settled in, Laurie and I, working as seasonal laborers, and saved up for land. Eventually, with plenty of help, we built a home, a log cabin of all things, not just logs but *juniper* logs full of oils ready to combust with the slightest urging. (I know. I know. We were dumb as dirt.) The house took my entire life savings, a heavy debt, and a year of hard labor to put up. My hair turned gray in a single summer. I thought: *I never want to do that again as long as I live.* I also thought: *I will never move away.*

That was years ago, before the fires started to grow so big, before we started hearing the not-so-subtle tone of commentators on national talk radio and editorialists in the *New York Times*:

move away, move away! The officials from the overhead team, who hold daily briefings, chew gum and run their fingers over their moustaches and kick at the dirt with lug soles, and I can read exasperation in their faces, too. *We would not have to bother,* they think, *if it weren't for you.*

That, too, is true enough. We live in the much-berated Wildland/Urban Interface, basically any development that abuts undeveloped land. (The acronym, WUI—pronounced WOO-eee!—makes this discussion sound a lot more fun than it is.) Protecting houses in the WUI has become a huge pain in the neck. I know. I used to fight fire, part-time, when I was a seasonal laborer. No one likes stringing out all that hose, setting up pumps by ramshackle trailers or log mansions. No one likes listening to the complaints of absentee owners, or worse, those yelling at you face to face: put it out, put it out! It's tiresome, if profitable, and it irks the philosophy minded among the firefighters because they would, frankly, rather let it burn. And they can't. Because of us.

Population estimates for the WUI vary wildly from thirty-four million in the lower forty-eight according to the 2000 census to one hundred forty million. What doesn't change is the forecast of doom: the number is growing and fast. If not for the many millions of us who live in the WUI, government agencies could manage fire differently, allow it to burn unhindered more often and do the work that fire should do. The United States Forest Service alone estimates it spends up to $1.2 billion a year protecting private structures even though only 14 percent of land adjacent to forests is developed. If more of it gets developed, firefighting costs will go up. That's a problem, I agree, one with plenty of large-scale solutions worth debating. Meanwhile, for me and others like me, the problem is small scale and a whole lot simpler. This is where we live. We are not moving. So, what can we do about it?

Me, I ran for public office. Not that there was much competition. No signs or slogans. In a town with a hundred year-round residents, it's hard to get three people, 3 percent of the population, to volunteer for anything as bureaucratic as this. So I ran unopposed and got elected along with two other commissioners, and come spring, we started work.

We trained a force of thirteen firefighters, a ragtag group of locals and seasonals, men and women, who survived forty hours of class work and power point presentations then passed the rigorous physical test—carrying forty-five pounds for three miles in forty-five minutes—and eventually donned bright yellow NoMex firefighter shirts. We did everything we were supposed to do. Or tried to. But it wasn't enough. There were still hoops to jump, boxes to check, certifications to achieve, and safety equipment to buy. There were so many meetings, so many rules, protocols established and maintained by none less than the Department of Homeland Security. Turned out the solution, like the problem, was bigger than we had ever imagined.

When lightning struck, a few volunteers showed up hoping to make a difference. We waited alongside paid firefighters at the local airstrip to be flown to remote locations we knew we could walk to easily enough, sometimes places we'd walked to before. But it was not to be. Official logic holds that air travel is safer, that firefighters would get worn out walking that distance, that a helicopter can do a size-up before putting anyone in danger. Moreover, managers explained, there were enough paid firefighters—twenty-something seasonals like I used to be, flirting and chomping brownies while waiting for the helicopters to arrive—that we weren't really needed.

As I backed my pickup away from the dusty airstrip, leaving my fate in the hands of others yet again, it was hard not to bristle like a four-year-old: *I can help.* It was harder yet to know I'd have to go back home—newly elected, bedecked in No-Mex—and say this: *there's nothing we can do.*

☙

Back at the work party, I try my best to hold the party line. But the situation has worsened. The day after we left the airstrip, while firefighters tried their damnedest, a burning snag broke off and rolled from atop a rocky cliff, and the fire took off, heading our way. I overhear a group of workers grumbling and decide to break in.

"They can't find a good place to put in a fire line," I say. "None of the drainages is wide enough or clear enough of vegetation. Maybe Arrow Creek. They say maybe Arrow Creek."

A few listeners chuckle with derision, frustration at fever pitch.

"They want to see all of this black," one says. He gestures at the scenery surrounding us—steep granite peaks forested green rise from lush green riverbanks—and shakes his head in disgust. He has a point. Every time fire managers speak to us at public meetings, they sound like evangelists. *Fire is good*, they say over and over. *Fire is good!* They're so intent on their message that—even though they've done a ton of fuel reduction work in the adjacent forest to protect our community, even though they more or less taught us how to do it—they forget to address the obvious. Fire is good for the forest, but not so good for houses.

"They'll bring in the big ships before it gets too close," I say. "I think they will protect us." And they will. Probably. As long as those resources, the big helicopters and air tankers, aren't busy working another higher-priority fire elsewhere in the state, or the nation.

My neighbor stares hard at me with something more like pity than anger, then he turns away.

I know what he's thinking, what he is trying not to say—god knows we are all trying, teeth gritted, to work together—he thinks they want us to move away.

We return to work in silence.

The one large-scale solution that seems unlikely is that we—all the many millions of us—will up and move. Where on earth would we all go? Still, the attitude is pervasive, and whether it's a firefighter's hard-earned fury or an eight-year-old's simple-minded shrug, it's a little hard to take. It's also hard to counter without getting defensive. Defensive in the liberal way, full of green excuses: *We recycle! We walk everywhere! We are not to blame!* Or in the conservative way, loud and chest thumping: *I worked hard. I deserve this. I pay taxes.* Or finally this, the truest of them all, the revolutionary way: if I move away, someone else will move in lickety-split and build a fancier house, a surgeon from Seattle, maybe, or a stockbroker from New York, or a billionaire preacher who will put in helicopter pads and hire bodyguards. In the end, *move away* usually means *make way for the rich people!*

I am not moving. I am dragging brush in the summer dusk.

The idea arose months ago, long before the lightning first struck, when already the purpose of the fire district seemed murky. What was the point in taxing ourselves, training ourselves, letting paperwork pile up like kindling, if we could effect so little change? Wasn't there something we could do? There was! We sent out letters to every property owner offering to do some work, any work, to help protect their place. We tacked a sign-up sheet in the post office, and right away, names appeared in ballpoint scrawl, and work began. We raked roofs, removed dead vegetation, thinned live vegetation, and pruned tree limbs. We were proud of it, and at one meeting, we bragged to a visiting state forester.

"We're creating a whole lot of defensible space."

"That's no way to think of it," he said.

"What do you mean?"

"When the Big One comes there might not be anybody around to defend these cabins. Not safely. You gotta think in terms of *survivable* space."

It was a sobering, if inarguable, point.

Bob has down-climbed the fir tree, and everyone is now dragging the heavy limbs across the yard. A cool breeze blows, and the river runs gray with glacial melt. A six-year-old tugs on her mother's leg to point out wild rose petals floating pink in an eddy. We're chatting as we work, about music and gardening, novels and backpacking trips, anything, anything but fire. There's laughter and camaraderie, the rare chance to spend time together in the busy tourist season. I'd like to say that it's all Amish barn-raising and square dance fun. But I don't want to romanticize it. Mostly it's just work, and for most of us it's work after work. Tonight, like most Monday nights, I am the youngest volunteer in attendance, save the kids dragged here by their folks. I am forty years old.

When I'm most discouraged I think the problem is that I arrived here too late. Too late for the fire-starved woods, and too late, I think, for a culture that had turned hard toward the city. Few earnest back-to-the-landers stake themselves out in rural America anymore. Those that do have a distinct political bent: anti-government, religious, protectionist. Environmentalists, for the most part, live in the city, and commute to the hills on weekends to recreate. By the time David Owens' landmark article appeared in the *New Yorker* in 2004 expounding Manhattan as the greenest place to live in America, the tide had turned. Those of us living in the woods were no longer nature lovers, just nature gobblers, living where we oughtn't.

Wildfire politics reinforce the stereotype. Pick up almost any book on the subject and you'll see what I mean. In *Wildfire and Americans*, former National Park Service director Roger Kennedy argues that people settle in the Wildland/Urban Interface because government essentially duped them into it with easy mortgages, cheap insurance, low taxes, and dispersed services. While this may be true for the outskirts, the exurban fringes of San Bernardino or Las Vegas, it couldn't be further from the truth for us. We have no easy mortgages, few services. Many of us don't even have fire insurance. It wasn't financial incentive that brought us here, and it certainly isn't financial incentive that keeps us here. It's nature, plain and simple, and our own selfish nature: wanting to be out here. And who knows? Maybe nature needs us, too.

This is what Wendell Berry has been arguing for decades: that we need to be stewards. The fire-starved woods are just one case in point. They're not likely to heal themselves. At this point, there are so many trees grown so tightly together that disease runs rampant and longer summers allow beetles to double hatch and do twice the damage. With so many diseased trees and so much accumulated underbrush, when the forest burns it burns so hot that even seeds that require fire to germinate may bake away. Natural regeneration becomes difficult or impossible. So this kind of thinning and clearing, lousy for profit but good for houses, is also good for the forest. When we hear arguments against thinning, they are against large-scale commercial thinning. No one debates this penny ante stuff. The only problem with the penny ante stuff is funding. There's no reliable market for very small-diameter logs, and getting them down and out of the woods is labor intensive. The alternative is to use taxpayer money, and there's not nearly enough to go around. Here in the tiny mountain valley, we have a near-perfect solution. We do the work for free. We use the wood to heat our homes.

Now I *am* romanticizing.

As the sun sets lower, smoke on the horizon creates a red orange collage, familiar to me from smoggy California, but a rare sight here. The beauty of it, for now, overshadows the danger. That and the work, which gets faster, more frenzied, as the end draws near. There's cold Gatorade on the cabin owner's porch and there's dinner waiting at home. I stop long enough to pull on a grubby sweatshirt and check my watch.

The burn piles tonight are growing higher than usual, higher probably than they ought to be.

A woman in her sixties stands poised to throw a twenty-foot-long limb. I race forward to help by tugging it onto the unwieldy stack. She yanks back angrily.

"I used to play semi-pro softball. Contrary to what people think, I can throw."

I hop back and watch her hurl the heavy branch high.

"Don't underestimate me," she says.

I smile.

"I never will again," I say.

I'm hoping that might apply to all of us, the fifteen of us here tonight and the many millions of us staked out in the WUI, disparaged and discouraged. We can do more than you think. More, even, than we think. When we're done affixing blame and wringing our hands, done analyzing history and zoning laws, done filling out forms and making computerized overlay maps and attending meetings, when we're done looking for market solutions or government grants or corporate donors, when it seems like there's not a damned thing left to do except move away, we can pick up a tool, any tool, and get to work.

Caucus

Drivers of road-worn Subarus, Izuzus, Toyotas, crept into the snow-
bermed parking lot, switched off the ignition, and took deep
breaths, each of us alone, before standing tall to enter. We weren't
afraid of what would happen inside, though we were certainly
curious, but we were plenty afraid of what would happen
outside. Everyone in town, driving by slowly, braking for the
ice-slick bridge over Rainbow Creek, would notice which cars
were parked in that lot. We imagined they would crane their
necks, roll their eyes, and tighten the grip on the steering wheel.
It shouldn't be any big deal, I know, to make your political
affiliation public in a free country, especially when your Toyota
or your girlfriend made it pretty obvious to start with. But a
big deal it was.

Before that day in 2004, holding a Democratic caucus here
seemed impossible to me, laughable, an oxymoron of sorts. The
town's image was of axe splitting and horse packing, cowboy
hats and round-hooded pickups from the 1940s. On the editorial
pages of regional newspapers Stehekin politics were celebrated
as quintessential Wild West: self-reliant, anti-government,
somewhere between *High Noon* and *Jeremiah Johnson*. Rumor
had it that there'd been Democratic caucuses back in the 1980s,
the not-too-distant past, but they'd been held at a private cabin
off the main drag, in the woods. Not right out in the open. This
time there'd be no hiding.

So, showing up at the first caucus felt a little like committing
treason and a little like coming out: shame, fear, and elation
rolled up in one.

It also felt, to me, like giving up. By 2004, we'd lived in town off and on for fourteen years, and through all those years I'd held fast to the idea that good Americans of every ilk are at heart the same. We believe in peace, freedom, family, and fairness. We appreciate healthy food and natural beauty. Above all, we live and let live. For years I'd clung to that ideal passionately. So much so that I went a tad overboard with empathy.

Over and over, in writing and at the dinner table, I'd defended so-called red state values. It wasn't even a stretch. After all, I believed in hard work and distrusted multicultural sensitivity and environmental hands-off-ishness. Who doesn't? I'd worked for the government long enough to bristle at the inefficiency. Closer to home, I worried sometimes that easy-going left-leaning folks like us could too easily become moochers: the kind of people who, say, never bring enough beer to a campfire. I even thought that the phrase "compassionate conservatism" made a lot of sense. I didn't vote that way, mind you, but I defended it the way you might defend a younger sibling, one who might be misguided but showed promise and needn't be dismissed out of hand. I believed more than anything in reasonableness.

Four years later, reasonableness had gone on the lam. Compassionate conservatism had turned to tax breaks for the richest of the rich. No Child Left Behind made the lives of every public school teacher I knew miserable, hopeless, very nearly insane. Government spying. War. Torture. Compare these to the sin of not bringing enough beer! Really, what could be worse?

Divisions at home, that's what. Differences deepened not just between members of our hundred-person community—there had always been those—but between friends. Politics seeped into our lives, like snowmelt into rock fissures, freezing and thawing over time until some friendships seemed ready to crack like granite. Tension grew at Friday Night Club. More and more topics turned off-limits until sometimes I preferred just to stay home. It used to be we could have civil disagreements around the campfire, hash things out, try to decide what to do about conflict in the Middle East, say, or about education or even—here, where it matters most—about the environment. Anymore we could not.

Maybe it was the fact that some neighbors hooked up satellite TVs and tuned into Fox News or, for that matter, others hooked up to the Internet and signed up with MoveOn.org. Maybe it was my fifteen-year-old nephew spouting heinous Ann Coulterisms in our kitchen while rolling meatballs. Or maybe it was me reaching middle age, cresting forty and turning predictably crotchety and unyielding.

And not just me. Easy-natured Laurie got in so many political spats that she took to listening to CSPAN all day, via satellite radio, as she pruned in the orchard. She rigged a rechargeable battery-powered speaker into a plastic four-gallon bucket to listen, trying to get the story straight, so to speak, from the horses' mouths.

If we'd bothered to notice, which we sometimes did, the community still stood together on local issues. Catastrophic fires and floods threatened the valley, alternating by season, and we helped each other out. An outsider arrived in the valley hawking telephone service, and we chased him off. Then there was the local road, our only road: we wanted it open! The Stehekin Valley Road—the ultimate road to nowhere since it was also *from* nowhere, inaccessible except by barge—had been grandfathered into the capital W Wilderness. When a major flood in fall 2003 tore out a major chunk, the only option for rebuilding would be an Act of Congress to redraw the Wilderness boundary, and Congress was otherwise disposed. We were out of luck.

I missed our road, pined for it even. Don't get me wrong: the downvalley portion of the road was intact, so we could get home just fine. Problem was, we couldn't get *away* from home. The upvalley portion of the road, the half that was now effectively cut off, had been our pathway into the mountains. In a day, you could access trailheads to glaciers and waterfalls and Zen-like peace or, if you preferred, you could hightail it from the same trailheads, twelve miles by foot, to the cross-state highway and head to the Fish Inn, a tavern that sold local brew, or to the Duck Brand, a restaurant that served a brick-sized wedge of mud pie smothered in hot fudge. The road took us away from small-valley politics. It took us away from each other. The road was our pressure relief valve. Now it was gone.

That winter I worked tearing down a government house scheduled for renovation and came home with my boot soles polka-dotted by carpet tacks that scratched our soft pine floors. On the radio, news from Iraq competed with speculation about the upcoming presidential election and discussions of the complicated fact that in Washington State the Democratic Party holds both a primary that counts for little and a caucus that counts for a lot. Everything seemed connected, and everything seemed screwed up, and so when I heard that a neighbor had gone to the trouble to organize a caucus in Stehekin I thought: Why not? It can't make anything worse. I bundled myself up, grabbed the ice scraper, and prepared to head out.

"You ready?" I called to Laurie.

"I'm not going," she said.

"What?"

She had other things to do. Sure, she was interested in educating herself about politics, but she saw no need to get carried away. No need for wrangling or taking sides. Not officially, at least. Not at nine o' clock on a Saturday morning.

"Come on," I said. "It's your patriotic duty."

"I'll be thinking of you while I read on the couch," she said.

I stomped off into the snow.

Outside the community hall, the sky remained gray, dark, shadowless, and cold, but inside, once we'd all arrived, the atmosphere warmed. We'd gathered here before for public meetings to listen to land managers in button-stretched uniform shirts, to county commissioners with flip charts. We'd considered alternatives and we'd tried to make sense, any sense, some *reasonable* sense of whatever was proposed, whatever might be foisted upon us next. This time it was different. I found myself growing hopeful, giddy even, fighting the urge, stone cold sober, to hug every person who walked in, pink cheeked, warm breath billowing.

A sign-in sheet on a folding table gave voters the option of committing to a candidate. Most people had checked: *Undecided.* I did the same. Proceedings began.

"I'm not sure if I'm a Democrat or Republican," said a local finish carpenter, a born-again Christian and a collector of vintage trail bikes. "What do these guys believe?"

"More fairness, you know, economically," someone explained.

"Which candidate will do the most about poverty?" asked a single mother of four.

One candidate stood out on that front, probably, everyone agreed. At least that's what he said. And what, exactly, could doing something about poverty entail? The minimum wage, we said, labor unions, food stamps.

We talked about the war.

"No blood for oil!" one outspoken eccentric neighbor cried, and others cringed. But we worked through that too. The conversation was a caricature, a regular idealized caucus.

We talked some more and voted once to a tie. Back to the drawing boards. We made some deals, trading candidate loyalties like brown bag lunch items. Peanut butter for tuna. Potato chips for a Ding Dong. My candidate won, and we sent our outspoken neighbor to the county convention as a delegate. And it was over.

I came home ecstatic.

"I can't believe you missed it," I told Laurie. "It was so cool."

This was it! At last! A group of people I agreed with, a club of sorts, a tribe, smaller than Stehekin, but bigger too, one that would allow me to feel: we're in this together. After the caucus, I began to ally myself more seriously and more strictly with liberal Democrats. I understood the irony, of course, that it had been precisely that belief that had sent me reeling. The Us-ness of flag waving conservatives. The Us-ness of anti-government types. But it didn't matter. I'd had it. I wanted to be Us. Without apologies.

Each evening at happy hour, while I waited for Laurie to get home from work, I sat on the porch with *The New Yorker* rereading Talk of the Town. Afternoon light filtered through cottonwood leaves. I switched on NPR and sipped a homebrew. This was not drinking alone, nothing like that, because as I read Hendrik Hertzberg, I felt camaraderie as strong as any I'd ever felt working on any trail crew. Politics became my secret tribe just as the Beatles, and all-things-Beatles, were to me when I was twelve. I was obsessed.

And I wasn't the only one. Choosing sides, like playground prep for a kickball game, took over everywhere we went downlake. Bookstores sported separate sections, right up front, for hardcover liberal screeds and conservative ones. I didn't know when it had happened or how I'd ended up in the middle of it, when, really, I lived so far on the fringe, away from it all. This was not reasonableness. It was Beatlemania. And I was swept up. I didn't know what else to do.

My neighbors did. They wanted the road reopened, and they planned to do something about it. Theirs was not so much grassroots politics, since there was nothing above the roots. They weren't a part of something big. They were the whole deal, something very small, miniscule, hardly noticeable. But they were unfazed. They pestered bureaucrats and lobbied congressmen. They wrote letters to editors, designed brochures, circulated petitions, and they did not tire, as one year passed, then another.

In early 2008, a local photographer planned a community photo that could be used to promote the cause. *We want our road!* The caption would read. *Please help us!* There hadn't been a community photo taken for ten years at least. It was getting harder to get everyone together, and especially this time of year—late winter, early spring. The photographer didn't mind. This was a new era. He figured he'd hold separate shoots and Photoshop us together. I tried not to think of this as metaphor. Laurie and I signed up, but before our day arrived, an email did.

The note came from a friend down the road who was deciding whether to pose in the photo. Our friend had lived here a long time. He'd raised his kids and driven the road grader, endured school board squabbles and floods, and once he'd watched his house burn down in ten minutes flat. He'd worked for the National Park Service, and since he retired he fixed everything from computers to backhoes. Sometimes he had a half dozen people lined up at his workshop, but he never turned anyone away. He rarely charged money, and when he did, it was not enough. If anyone was a card-carrying member of the capital C Community, Mr. Fix-it was. But he was also a realist. And on that day he was looking for an ally.

What do you think of opening the road, really?

He was thinking of the waste of time and money, and the philosophical problem, too: a road in Wilderness is an oxymoron. I understood his points, maybe even agreed with them, but it didn't matter. I had long since decided: I was part of the community and the community wanted the road open, so I wanted the road open.

The reply I sent was sheepish and tongue-in-cheek and not terribly clear:

Why not? What's wrong with reopening a road into
Wilderness that benefits a hundred people and has a seven-
figure price tag? Would you rather spend that money in Iraq?
Mr. Fix-it's instant response was exuberant.

I thought I was the only one who thought this way! His message
zipped twenty-four thousand miles into space and back from
his house two miles down the dirt road to mine. *Now we can
have a club!*

I was in a quandary. He'd misunderstood. I hadn't meant to
agree with him, even though I kind of did. I sat at the keyboard,
fingers hovering, thinking: I can do this, go against the grain.
Thinking: I want to be in the reasonable club. But also thinking
this: I can't. I just can't. While I considered how best to respond,
composing and re-composing in my mind, a new message
popped onto the screen. Mr. Fix-it had figured it out.

Sorry. I guess I misread.

By now, email did not seem the proper forum. I hopped in
the truck and drove down to his workshop where, for once, no
one was waiting. He smiled as he saw me approach and threw
an arm around my shoulder.

"I guess we're not in any club. Except the special love club,"
he said.

Not long afterward, Laurie and I prepared to go to the
Democratic caucus: my second, since I'd gone in '04, Laurie's
first ever. The morning was sunny, easily the sunniest morning
we'd had in four months, and our mood was almost impossibly
hopeful. What wasn't there to be hopeful about? Two fine
candidates: a black man, and white woman, both smart and gutsy
and compassionate. And the road—the section we really needed,
the section we still had—which had frozen hard in November,
was melting out at last. Things were looking up.

So up, in fact, that I hadn't bothered to decide who to vote for.
I liked Obama. I'd tear up at his speeches. But I also didn't know

much about him. Hillary sounded reasonable, too. Her eyebrows pinched extra much, I thought, and there was something in her speech making that sounded insincere. I distrusted her association with those super-fat Clinton years, all that stock market euphoria, and mostly I could not forgive her vote in favor of the Iraq War. But her policies made sense, and anyway weren't we all on the same team? Who cared who won? I might just come and go *Undecided*, I thought.

But I didn't. As soon as Laurie and I walked in, the trouble began. Again, as in '04, there was a nice warm fire. Again, a cheery crowd bundled in layers of snow wear—colorful hand-knitted hats and down coats, scarves and snow boots. I signed in: name, address, date of birth. The final column asked which candidate you were there to support. I paused. I was not even required to fill in that blank. But what the heck? Like a guy pulling up a stool at a sports bar and picking a team to root for because it makes the game more fun to watch, I wrote: Obama.

We sat side by side, Laurie and I, and the discussion began. A retired schoolteacher, a newcomer since the last go round, started the ball rolling with No Child Left Behind. Then came the messy stuff: the war, torture, lying, spying.

Right away, it became apparent that the Clinton supporters had come prepared. They had talking points and printouts, and this annoyed me. When the tally was taken, as in '04, we were split right down the middle. Six for Obama. Six for Clinton. Two for Kucinich. Now I was getting seriously agitated, fidgety, and impatient. If not for the so-small crowd, I'd probably have been rolling my eyes or whispering to Laurie. I did not remember this from that chummy first go-round, four years earlier. I did not like it. This gathering felt exactly like junior high: all attitude and posturing. Not that anyone was acting that way. Except maybe me.

I spoke up loudly, awkwardly, babbling about Clinton's pinched eyebrows and her seeming insincerity. Meanwhile, my own eyebrows were pinched, my arguments thin, my attitude snotty. We wrangled until one Kucinich voter vowed to switch to Obama. The other would stay undecided, she said. I sat back satisfied.

Was everyone ready? The moderator asked.

We were ready.

We voted again: Clinton seven. Obama six. One undecided.

This couldn't be. I felt broadsided, betrayed. Not because my candidate had lost or because I had realized too late who my candidate was, but because I realized I didn't have a tribe, no clique to sit with in the lunch room and think: here, at last, I am at home. I had thought we were in this together. But we weren't. Not really. It was precisely the same mistake I'd made so many years before when I believed that we in Stehekin were a special club, immune to the divisions of the outside world. Now that seemed laughable. Ridiculous. On the way home, Laurie drove and chattered about how fun the experience had been. I felt adrift. I would have preferred to go home and pout. But I couldn't.

I'd made a plan to stop by and help Jonathan with a new tool, a grip hoist, he'd purchased for rolling large logs onto his portable lumber mill. I also wanted to look at some pine slab, eighteen inches wide, two inches thick, that we might like to buy to use atop a bookcase we were building. Jonathan had milled the slab from a tree removed in a canyon downlake. He had dried it carefully, steadily, over time, stacking it with weight and proper air space, and now he had it stored on end in the basement by the woodstove and the television where his wife Jean often watched episodes of *Sex in the City* while preparing organic garden vegetables for canning. That winter we'd all been watching *The Wire*. On long skis into the woods, miles from anywhere, our tribe had been a bunch of imaginary drug dealers in Baltimore. Now as a break from politics, we returned there.

"Stringer Bell turned out to be a bastard, didn't he?" Jonathan said.

We laughed again and talked about Bubbles, the snitch, and we grew animated again, post-caucus, on a sun-drenched afternoon. By the time we got around to complaining about the caucus, it didn't seem like as big a deal. We began to revisit the morning, the intrigue of it. Who might have switched from Obama to Clinton? Who? We recounted and speculated. We drank a shot of whiskey—why not?—and speculated again. This was as fun as *The Wire*.

By the end of the visit, we were surer about Obama, surer about almost everything. We had no idea, still, who might have switched, but in our sunlit basement buzz, we were completely one hundred percent for each other. We were Us. They, the vote changer, the wishy washers, the Clinton supporters were Them: the Stringer Bells, the deceivers of the world. Yeah yeah. This was it. Our own special club, we were, and it felt right and good. I stepped back out into the sunshine, eager to get home to Laurie.

I crashed through the door, and didn't even wait to remove my boots before I began revisiting the caucus, explaining who must've voted for whom. Who could've switched? Who would've? I started to go over the count again. I don't get it. Who changed from Obama to Clinton? Who could be that stupid?

"I did," Laurie said.

"You did?"

"I did."

Fading sunlight played yellow on our dented pine floor, soft and imperfect. Dust settled on books on the unfinished shelves and in the cracks in the plastic cases of my long-neglected Beatles cassettes. My allegiances—to writers and rock stars, to philosophies and ideologies—didn't sway, but they didn't mean as much. Whatever Zen-like peace I used to find driving up the road to the mountains, away from the tensions and conflicts, I'd have to find at home. So I laughed and opened a beer. And toasted Laurie. Turns out we don't have a club. There is no club. Except the special love club.

The Seam

On the day of Roberta's funeral, Laurie and I loitered outside the bible church as long as we could. We'd ridden down Lake Chelan from our land-locked town of a hundred people—now minus one— on a private boat with six friends, then changed clothes in the bathroom at the brand new Starbucks before driving the winding lakeside highway past the hillside orchards, to this church where the ceremony would be held, the church her widower, Don, had chosen. But Laurie and I didn't want to go in. We waited until we could wait no more, staring out at the lake, sun glinted and glassy blue, so seemingly benign.

When at last we peeled off our sunglasses and garnered our courage, we stepped through the door into a wide, boxy, and windowless room. Multi-colored tapestries hung from white walls, two stories tall. Rejoice! one read. Praise! said the other. Plastic chairs, three hundred of them, sat in rows. A heavyset man in a suit leaned against the podium with an acoustic guitar slung backwards over one shoulder.

The scene was familiar and unfamiliar. Laurie and I had separate religious upbringings, hers Baptist, mine Catholic, but the experience was much the same: liberal politics with conservative accoutrements. Eco-theology with steeples and a pipe organ for her. No-Nukes with stained glass and a crucifix for me. Here the pattern was reversed: conservative politics with liberal accoutrements. Creationism with guitar hymns. Family values with rainbow praise banners. And there was something disconcerting about seeing everyone here. Not just

159

the predictable discomfort of, say, heavy-equipment operators in dress slacks or tomboys in heels, but their easiness, too. The regular churchgoers among us crowded into the middle rows. Laurie and I took two seats in an empty row near the back and off to the left.

The casket sat front and center, raised high and draped in roses.

Laurie sucked in her breath.

"What if it's open?" she asked.

"Look," I said. "The lid is closed."

"They might open it."

"You don't have to look if you don't want to," I said.

Funerals were my expertise, maybe because of Catholicism—generations of Latin rosaries and hard-drinking wakes in my blood—but mostly because of plain hard luck. I'd been to my father's and I'd been to my grandmother's, and most recently, the previous fall, I'd traveled back home to California for yet another. A friend's husband had dropped dead of a heart attack atop the roof of their vacation home. He was forty-two, in perfect health, and I heard the news via email on the hangover morning after singing karaoke late into the night in Wallace, Idaho.

From a gas station along the interstate, I called a close mutual friend or, I should say, a formerly close friend. For years we'd tried to reconnect, but she attended an evangelical church in my suburban hometown and I lived openly with a woman out in the boonies, and the chasm between us had grown impossibly wide, dicey to cross. Now, suddenly, none of that mattered. I stood at a pay phone, the wind howling across the scablands, a stray dog chasing silver food wrappers among the weeds.

"What should I do?" I asked. Nothing, I thought she'd say. There's nothing you can do.

She didn't reply.

"Should I come down?" I asked.

"That's up to you," she said.

"There will be a lot of people there," I said.

"You're not a lot of people," she said.

The line fell silent. I could see Laurie waiting, hair whipping, and I could see the dog scrounging, and even though what my evangelical friend said made no sense at all, grammatically or otherwise, I knew exactly what she meant. What a lot of people do or don't do doesn't matter. What *you* do matters.

I booked a flight and left work mid-project, reconstructing a historic wooden flume, and flew south, ditching work boots for city clothes, and arrived at the door with a bagful of groceries and a flower bouquet. There were other people there, many of them, mingling, playing with my friend's two young kids. There were other sacks of groceries and bouquets of flowers, too, and I thought immediately: I did not need to come. Then my friend appeared. She collapsed on the couch and sobbed for a very long time, and I tried to comfort her. She said she wasn't hungry, and I talked her into eating one grape at a time, and she laughed at last, a little. We took a long slow walk, just the two of us, around the block. She wore flip-flops and folded her arms tight across her mid-section as though trying to hold it all in, where it belonged, where it wouldn't stay, not for a very long time. We talked about her husband. We talked about her kids. We talked about God and how we didn't get Him—Her, It—at all. I moved from my mom's house to her house, to help with meals and waking the kids for school, then walking more circles in warm November rain through traffic splatters on wide empty sidewalks between asphalt and chain link fences. No trees. No grass. No answers. I didn't need to come, but I was glad that I had.

On the plane home, I put on headphones and stared out the window and wept. In the aisle seat, a jolly long-bearded fellow with orange logger suspenders ordered drinks by the fistful. Tiny Johnnie Walker bottles clattered and collected. He drank. I cried.

I cried so hard, at some point, watching the coastline below, soft blue unfurling against brown, a long hazy seam, that my nose began to bleed, and I did not have a Kleenex, and I did not want to ask, so I used a piece of notebook paper, absorbency zero. A woman sitting in the row in front of me buzzed the flight attendant ("We've got a bleeder," she announced) who brought me Kleenex so I could clean myself up, and the drunken stranger stared hard. When the wheels hit the ground, bouncing, he turned to me.

"Whatever is hurting you," he said. "It's going to be OK. I am a minister of the Universal Life Church." He reached across the armrests and the empty seat between us, offering his hand.

I smiled.

The Universal Life Church is the click-yes church, the one that will make you a minister online. I knew since I'd done it myself so that I could officiate at a friend's wedding. After you're ordained, you're transferred to a screen where you may choose to learn a) more about the precepts of the church or b) more about the tax benefits of being ordained. I clicked neither. Just returned to regular life.

I thought I might tell my seatmate: Me, too. Instead, I held his hand briefly and thanked him earnestly, then stooped into the aisle to pass through the tunnel into the terminal and on. This, I think, is how it goes: you hover over the place where water laps at the edge of a continent, seemingly moving forward, encroaching, but it's not. The seam holds. The plane lands. You head to baggage claim, and you return to lugging rough-sawn timbers on your shoulder and felling alders with a chainsaw and a rope winch and the glory of cold sweat drying, and it's over. Until it's not.

❧

Another plane. A de Havilland Beaver, a six-seater, taxied from a small airport on a high bluff over the Columbia River and headed uplake for a water landing on floats. The addition of wheels, the ability to use an airport for takeoffs and landings, was a new development for the company, which had been in operation on Lake Chelan since the 1940s, now under new ownership. The change had been billed as progress: More options! Late Saturday afternoon, the plane flew low and near the forested hillsides, as it always had, the lake a wide rift below, sun slits on the water, and no boats this time of year, too early, and no forest fires either. Drift collected in brown swaths, more visible from the air than it would be from a boat. Uprooted trees and broken limbs. Propeller bait. The river had been running near flood stage for a week, flushing debris down side creeks, too, and you could see this, the danger, from the air, but you could also see the late snow on the mountains, pink tinged in the afternoon light.

Roberta had been running errands and had brought a fifteen-year-old neighbor girl along with her to drive since, now in her mid-sixties, her vision was failing from diabetes. (Who knew this? We did not know this.) They chose to fly home because they wanted to be back in time for the annual Trillium Festival, where locals played music and recited poetry and shared a potluck, the first of the season, at the one-room school. Not to be missed. Summer home owners, a doctor and his wife, now on the plane, had traveled from Spokane for the same reason. The Trillium Festival is a big deal, and inside the plane, the passengers chattered excitedly. They descended toward the water, as they always did, toward the blunt forest edge at the head of the lake, and the dock, and the waiting crowd at the schoolhouse, and as they did, a man standing alone at a small cabin on a cliff edge, a few short miles from town, raced for a radio. He'd seen the wheels down un-retracted and tried to call anyone who could alert the pilot. Too late. The plane hit, wheels spinning, and flipped end over end, into thirty-eight-degree water. It could not, after that, have taken long.

$$\mathcal{C}$$

Back in the church, the local downlake fire chief sat beside Laurie and me. The accident had been so unexpected, so jarring that, I suppose, he thought he'd show up to support the community. Then came Jean and Jonathan, then Shari and Bob from across the road. We'd helped slop out their house after the big flood, hauling armfuls of soaked paperbacks and throw rugs out to the yard. In front of us, Renee sat with two of her kids, Ursula and Aaron. Aaron at eight was a big-eyed boy who passed out napkins at potlucks and asked for bagpipes for Christmas. Ursula, twelve, wore oversized boys' plaid shirts, a style all her own. When we told her how cute she looked, she shrugged and said she wanted "to look like Fern" from *Charlotte's Web*, and how sweet, how impossibly sweet, to know a pre-teen who dresses after a book you read when you were young. Less sweet to have to share with her the first funeral of someone she loved.

Across the room, we could see another teenaged girl, the one who had escaped the submerged plane, sitting now between her parents. The teenager had managed to get out, and the pilot got out, and the doctor's wife got out. The doctor's wife had felt her husband shove her toward safety and felt certain that he'd follow close behind. Only he didn't. Of five aboard, three survived. Now the teenager sat surrounded by well-wishers in the bible church; she nodded, smiled, fidgeted, returned hugs, looked around the room, and adjusted her skirt. Astonished, no doubt. Who among us was not astonished?

"Was your dad's open?" Laurie asked.

I nodded.

"Did you look?"

I nodded again.

Laurie's hand rested in mine. Not long ago, this would have been a big deal for us, holding hands in front of so many people. Now it came easy, not the point of anything. The only point was that Roberta was gone, and we were sad. The photo on the program had caught us off guard. She could be a stern woman, Roberta: tall and broad handed, the epitome of a farm woman, with a gray bun and glasses. Since joining the Pentecostal church in the 1980s, she wore the same type of outfit most days: button-up blouses and long denim skirts, tennis shoes and socks. Everything about her manner said this: no nonsense.

"Roberta can be intimidating," I once told Laurie. "That scowl."

"You scowl like that, too," she said. "You shouldn't scowl when you're out running along the road. Just make yourself smile when you wave at passing cars."

"I don't have to. I don't have to put on a show just because of where we live."

"You don't have to think about it that way. You can just be nice."

Or, it turned out, I could be not-nice or at least not-fake. Roberta's blunt manner seemed, after that, like permission. Like relief.

But the photo on the funeral program showed something more. One of Roberta's eyebrows lifted ever so slightly higher than the other, as if in response to a question or an inside joke. Delighted. She looked delighted. I'd seen that look before: in the garden, in the post office, at the craft shop, all Roberta's haunts. I'd seen it the first day I worked in the one-room school ten years earlier.

I'd planned a grammar lesson complete with dangling participles for the eighth graders, solid writers, smart kids, without a whit of understanding of sentence structure. Nouns, verbs, they got that much. Beyond that, they were in trouble.

As a part-time instructor, I only dropped in and never had full responsibility for the class. The schoolteacher was away, and on this particular day Roberta, the superintendent, was substituting. I launched into my spiel, and Roberta, in the back of the room, lifted one eyebrow slightly and nodded once slowly, and mid-lecture I was grateful to the nuns who'd taught me to diagram sentences twenty years earlier, and for the chance to pass the skill on, and mostly, for Roberta's evident approval. She was a woman who approved of rigor.

For several years Roberta taught kindergarten—the one-room school had, for a long time, been two: one room for grades one through eight, one for the "readiness" kids, the kindergarteners—and mid-way through one school year, she gave it up.

"Which teacher do you like best?" a mother asked her young son, Dylan, who was in that class.

Dylan mentioned the new teacher and how much fun she was.

"Yes, but which teacher do you learn more from?" his mother asked.

"Roberta," said the five-year-old. "Roberta's harder, but she's better."

You didn't need an explanation any more long-winded than that.

❧

A week before the funeral, Roberta and I had worked together planting her garden. The sun was bright, the newly tilled soil warm. We pounded in the fence posts and tied them with rag strips. We measured the rows with tape measures and pulled out a string line, and she handed me the seed packets. I did not know why. I didn't know about her failing vision, and didn't want this responsibility, but I also did not argue, ever, with

Roberta. I knelt down, and held the seeds in my palm, and set them carefully one by one in the soil: cabbage, lettuce, radish, chard. We had no broccoli seeds, but she was planning to go downlake, and so was I, and one of us could pick up a packet of seeds. One of us would. We left it at that. At lunch, she asked how long I planned to work, and I said that was it. I had things I had to do. That was it.

Now people were suggesting we take over the garden, Laurie and I, that Don would need someone. This was ridiculous, I thought. How could we be the ones? Don knew everything about gardening, and we knew nothing. Besides, there were many other people who knew him better, who belonged to the church. A meal chain had been organized and we weren't even on the list. Surely someone else would step up.

To say that Roberta's politics were not like ours would be an understatement. Not that she ever told me as much. We never spoke of politics, outside of small-town politics, and even then with considerable restraint. We did with her husband, Don, sure. As postmaster, before he retired, he gave frequent mini-speeches on the illegality of the federal income tax and the inevitability of one-world government. Other than the fact that Roberta had once greeted Newt Gingrich's arrival in the valley with exuberance, her beliefs went unspoken. As did ours. And that creates tension of its own.

Another school year. Research papers this time. The kids had chosen their topics, and Dylan, now an eighth grader, had chosen the Iraq War. He'd overheard too many adult conversations, I feared, in the nearby liberal Lutheran community where his father worked.

"That will be a hard topic," I said.

"But it's important that I understand it," he said.

"OK," I said.

On the final day of the project, the day for oral presentations, the teacher was gone, and Roberta, the substitute, did not look amused. She stared out the windows and scowled, while Dylan muddled through Sunnis and Shiites as best he could. She made no eye contact with him, none with me, as he slipped in the word: pre-emptive. She sat straight backed and unmoving through the presentations until everyone was finished, then she spoke directly to me.

"Ana Maria, do you have a teaching certificate?" she asked.

I'd been working at that school by then for a decade for a pittance, taking time from my writing and real paying jobs, and she was going to challenge me now, right in front of the kids. I was angry.

"I don't. I have a Masters Degree, but no certificate."

"That's too bad," she said. "Because you're so good with these kids. I'm so sick today with the flu I should be at home. I wish someone else could fill in."

Turns out, she wasn't mad. She was sick. And she'd said what she said in front of the kids as a compliment. They'd all hear it and go home to tell their folks.

The tension, however big or small, never subsides. No matter how long we stay, I'm convinced it will never subside: the feeling of un-belongingness, the sense that who you are or what you believe is, on some level, suspect. The stories we like to tell best are the ones where the divide—religious, political, cultural—is breached. And there are many. But most of the time, with most people, the divide holds. Respect for the divide—the fact that we all understand and accept it—is, in no small part, what keeps life in a small town peaceable.

Still, Roberta had been our friend. And it started, as many friendships do, over food. Laurie and I had both been vegetarians for a short time in our twenties but we'd given it up. ("Everyone's a vegetarian when they're twenty-three," one friend always quips.) Then, suddenly, in her early forties, Laurie had a moral crisis. If she was going to eat animals, she thought, she should at least kill them herself. She considered deer hunting, but that would take a serious commitment. So she decided to start small. She asked Don and Roberta if she could help them butcher chickens. If they found this request odd, they didn't say as much. Don handed her the axe to do the deed, then she carried the bird inside to pluck and gut with Roberta. And so the day went. The set-up was immaculate: newspaper spread, knives sharpened. Buckets on the floor collected feathers and feet and guts to be buried in the garden: free fertilizer. Stainless steel bowls on the counter filled with livers and hearts and gizzards to be canned: dog treats for the winter. The smell, Laurie reported, was horrific, the process fascinating. I came home from a day out working, maintaining hiking trails.

"Well, are we eating chicken or tofu?" I asked.

"Tofu tonight, chicken tomorrow," she said.

For the next few years we'd butcher chickens in October, a full-day affair, with Don and Roberta in exchange for meat. And not just meat. One summer, Roberta sent us a note offering produce from her garden, the extra stuff, for five bucks a box. No matter what was in the box, it had to be worth five bucks, so I showed up one afternoon and came home with carrots, cabbage, basil, broccoli, beets, chard. The next week there was more: green beans, tomatoes, corn, jalapeños. To grow these things in a flood-prone glacial valley requires years of commitment, building the soil wheelbarrow by wheelbarrow. Laurie and I had gardened down on the low ground of our property when we first arrived in the valley, but that washed away, deer fence and all. Not once or twice. Three times. That was it. We started the process on high ground, up on the rocky bluff, but it was likely to take years. So, I began to visit Roberta every week.

One day in the coat room at school, Roberta reminded me to stop by.

"Before I get any more food from you, Roberta, I'd better start helping you weed," I said.

"Would you?" she cried. She clapped her hands together. It was as animated as I'd ever seen her. "I didn't want to ask."

"Yeah, well, otherwise it's like The Little Red Hen. You know, nobody helps until it's time to eat."

Roberta laughed, nodded: "*Not I, said the cat,*" she said.

She did know.

After that, I began to show up.

Dylan, now a high school senior, college bound in fall, sat in the bible church. So did the owner of the local hardware store, two of the ferry pilots, several former park rangers, dozens of former Stehekin School students. Two of them, Brun and Seth, men now in their thirties, sat beside their mothers, having traveled across the state on a work day, leaving their own families at home. Laurie tapped me on the arm to point out Tony. Before his divorce, Tony had been our land partner, our quiet steady land partner, the snow shoveler, the well-pump repairer, always with his Cubs hat on and a crossword half-finished on the kitchen table. He no longer lived in the small town full-time, but here he came, hatless, in a dress shirt.

Eventually, Laurie and I stopped nudging and pointing. It was clear enough that we knew nearly everyone in the church, and we had a story to tell about every one of them, and they'd all die sooner or later, and we would show up again. Just as when we die, they'll show up. I'd always known that someone would be there in a pinch, in a flood or a fire, or if we ran out of canning jars, or when the truck needed a jump start. I hadn't thought enough about the ties growing stronger than that, thick and sinewy, as reliable as they are taut.

The local Pentecostal minister, who works with us on the volunteer fire district, stood and prayed. The guitar player crooned a hymn of sorts, a personalized love song, James Taylor-esque, not far from what I used to hear at Mass in the seventies, and the schoolteacher gave the eulogy, a fine tribute about Roberta's legacy as a community pillar—at the school, as substitute postmaster, as head of the craft cooperative, secretary of the property owners' association—and about how the accident, the shock of it, had affected us all, brought us closer, made us more grateful for each other. I thought about how in another era I would not even have shown up. That era was over. It had been over, in fact, for a very long time.

At the end of the service, the casket lid was flipped open.

Laurie turned to me.

"You don't have to go," I said.

"Are you going?"

"I don't know," I said.

The ushers stepped back row by row to invite guests forward, somber and orderly. We watched as half the attendees turned to leave. They walked, heads down, toward the back of the church and out into the sun. Others, the older folks among us, stayed put. People in their seventies who had been in their fifties when we arrived were now sun weathered and stooped, work worn and serious, religious and not. They walked slowly, paused by the casket and walked back down the aisle. Nothing to it.

Laurie and I weren't home the day the plane went down. We'd traveled downlake for a conference, though some suspected that we had done it to avoid the Trillium Festival: the amateur music, the stumbling poetry recitations, the forced socializing. They were partly right. We were sitting at a café downlake, checking email, when we received the instant message. *Hurry. We need your help.* And there is no more helpless feeling in the world than to hear those words. *Hurry. We need your help.* Except to hear this: *it's Roberta.*

They dove. So many of them. They saw the plane upside down and dove. Thirty-eight-degree water, and our friends dove, fully clothed. They performed CPR, some for the first time in their lives, on people they knew and loved, and they did it for two hours, on small boats skimming down the lake racing for civilization and waiting for paramedics to make a determination, even though they already knew. Still, they could not stop. Two bodies. Two boats. Twelve responders. Some people prayed, and some did compressions; others just drove the boats. Why? Why did they do it? Why does anyone do it? Because it's right or because it's hard wired in the brain? You do it without a thought: you're in that cold water, and you're entering the fuselage, and there they are, the bodies. One still belted upside down, pinned in place, one floating prone, and you can't get them out, because you are too cold and you need a breath, and it's dark as hell, and for weeks you'll stay up all night, sleepless, agonizing because you should have done more or you could have done it better, and there is no comfort. All you know is that the edge is still there, the seam where life meets death, and how you behave on that seam is all reflex, and probably a measure of how you behaved the whole time.

"Will you come with me?" Laurie asked.

I nodded.

We stood and walked up the aisle, side by side, not hand in hand. I reached to shake the minister's hand, and he leaned in to hug me, and I could feel the divide dissolving fast. Laurie had passed the casket, and so it was my turn to glance down into the pink satin, the bloated face, powdered thick and white, looking more like a poorly formed wax figure at Fisherman's Wharf than our friend. By the time I looked up, I could see Laurie hurrying toward the door, toward the sunshine, to more small talk, hand shaking, hugs, and the sun now angling downward, the lake in the shade.

"I hear you're taking over the garden. Pretty big shoes to fill," the schoolteacher said to me as I emerged. Roberta was a half foot taller than I am. She must've worn size thirteen easy. "What do you got?" he asked.

I stood on one foot to show him.

"Seven," I said.

He clucked his tongue as if to say: might not be enough.

"Well, seven and a half," I said.

He reached for my hand and shook it.

A few days later we'd stop by Don's, and he'd hand me a small soggy packet. I'd forgotten all about buying broccoli seeds. But, of course, Roberta hadn't. She'd carried these with her onto the plane.

"They're a little wet," Don said.

I took them, and together Laurie and I put them in the ground.

The summer grew long, the broccoli plants tall, twenty of them with heads a foot in diameter and shoots going wild. The pace accelerated: blanching, freezing, canning, resting on the porch, coffee in hand, talking with Don, or not talking, just sitting together, the porch swing squeaking, the birds chirping. Swallows nested under the eaves, taunting the house cats. Deer got to the strawberries. Bears got the grapes. The chicks arrived in a cardboard box, peeping loudly, in June, and we butchered them in the fall. At first, I could not recognize the flowers Roberta had had me plant when they sprouted tiny as pinky nails, but

I knelt in the soft dirt, picking between them and among them, playing God, and by late summer a jungle of color—zinnias, marigolds, bachelor buttons, cosmos—grew tall as my waist, over my head, blooming.

After the funeral, we did not yet know what had hit us or what was to come. We did not yet know a damned thing. We skipped the cemetery and stopped instead for store-bought veggies to load into five-gallon buckets and haul uplake on our friends' boat. Laurie sat in the hold and played cards. I stood on tiptoes beside the boat pilot, a pallbearer, watching for drift floating on the water. Swerve left. Swerve right. We'd make it home safe by dinnertime and climb the ramp from the dock to dry ground.

Acknowledgements

Many of these essays have been previously published. I am grateful to the editors at the journals that published them:

"Potluck." *Open Spaces: Views from the Northwest* Volume 8 Issue 1, 2005.

"Thirteen Percent Catholic." *Pilgrimage* Volume 32 Issue 1, Spring 2007.

"*La Linea.*" *Pilgrimage* Volume 30 Issue 2, Summer 2005.

"*La Linea.*" (Reprint) In *Telling it Real: The Best of Pilgrimage 2003-2008*. Edited by Peter Anderson. Pilgrimage Press. 2010.

"Sand-Calloused Places." *Mountain Gazette* 135, September 2007.

"The Fall Line." *Mountain Gazette* 151, February 2009.

"This, Jack London Reminded Me." *Mountain Gazette* 118, October 2005.

"What's Heaven without a Gate?" *Weber Studies* Volume 22 Number 3, Spring/Summer 2006.

"Lost and Found." *Mountain Gazette* 120, January 2006.

"The Woman Who Gardens With Bears." In *Wild Moments: Adventures with Animals of the North*. Edited by Michael Engelhard. University of Alaska Press. 2009.

"Spawning in Mud." *Watershed* 7, Spring/Summer 2009.

"Spawning in Mud." (Reprint) *Writing Nature*, 2010.

"Defensible Space" as "Just Right Here." *Oregon Quarterly*, Summer 2009.

"Caucus." *North American Review* Volume 294 Numbers 3-4, May-August 2009.

"The Seam." *Under the Sun* Volume XIV Number 1, Summer 2009.

Notes:

Two paragraphs of "Thirteen Percent Catholic" also appeared in *Test Ride on the Sunnyland Bus: A Daughter's Civil Rights Journey*. University of Nebraska Press. 2010.

An essay titled "Saw Chips in My Bra"—unrelated to the essay
in this collection—also appeared in *A Mile in Her Boots: Women
Who Work in the Wild*. Edited by Jennifer Bove. Travelers
Tales. 2006.

Special thanks to M. John Fayhee at *Mountain Gazette*, tireless
champion of small-time scribblers all around the West.

Thanks to Linda Cooper, David Oates, Michelle Nijhuis
who read the manuscript and offered keen insight and helpful
suggestions. And to Laurie Thompson who served as both fact
checker and memory aid with humor, compassion, wisdom,
and a whole lot of courage.

Thanks to Karen Leona Anderson, Jerry Gabriel, and the
faculty of St. Mary's College of Maryland for providing me
time and space at the Artist House—many necessary miles
from home—where I completed the final two essays.

Thanks to Mary Elizabeth Braun at Oregon State University
Press for patiently shepherding the book to publication.

We've had a hard spell of loss in recent years. Among
those I remember daily with great fondness and respect are
those who appear in these pages: Father Dominic DePasquale,
Walter G. Winkel, Roberta Pitts, and Phil Garfoot.

My most sincere gratitude, finally, to my friends and
neighbors in Stehekin—those still here and those who have
moved on—without whom I'd be seriously lost.